Worth It: A Journey to Food & Body Freedom

6 Essential Steps to Ditching the Diets &
Nourishing Your Body from the Inside Out

Katy Weber

Praise for **Worth It: A Journey to Food & Body Freedom**

"Katy weaves a relatable personal narrative about her own relationship with food and weight with digestible summaries of some critical aspects of the non-diet approach. Referencing some of the greatest thought leaders in this space — including Linda Bacon, Ellyn Satter, and others — this book reads like a juicy memoir with self-help benefits. If you're still struggling with dieting, you will definitely see yourself in this book ... and hopefully, a path to another way of living."

— Isabel Foxen Duke, anti-diet coach
and emotional-eating expert

"*Worth It* is 130 pages of recovery, truth, and evidence-based expertise about how and why overcoming chronic dieting will provide you with liberation in your life. The author has done an exceptional job at inviting you in to her experiences and weaving in facts throughout the entire book about the dangers of weight-focus and how to move toward freedom from dieting. She brings a valuable and credible approach to how you can overcome disordered thinking about food, movement and your body. This is a fantastic read for anyone who struggles with eating and body image."

— Sumner Brooks, MPS, RDN, LD,
author of *Savvy Girl: A Guide to Eating*

"I needed this book more than I ever knew. When it comes to what we eat, what we weigh and how we look, Katy Weber boldly exposes what most women think in our heads but are too afraid to say out loud. In sharing it here, those thoughts finally feel less daunting. *Worth It* is a testament to what happens when you face your biggest fear and let yourself go. Beauty. Relief. True fullness and self love."

— Lauree Ostrofsky, author of *Simply Leap* and *I'm Scared & Doing It Anyway*

"*Worth It* is a revolutionary and refreshingly honest guide to reclaim true health and wellness, and it has nothing to do with a certain size or weight! This book exposes the insanity of the diet industry, while giving the reader an immediate and practical action plan based on self love and care. Worth It is a powerful read for anyone, but if you are a mother, it is a must read now!"

— Peggy Belles, author of *Peace in Pieces: A Memoir Told Through Poetry*

Praise for **Worth It with Katy**

"I cannot say enough great things about Worth It with Katy! It's so tempting to 'go on a diet,' but after years and years of that failing again and again, I finally tried something new — Katy saved my sanity and my health!"

— Sheila

"Katy offers the perspective of someone who has 'been there' but has achieved what many of us have been trained to believe is unobtainable."

— Sara

"What Katy offers is not a weight loss program, it's a judgment loss program. She teaches you how to stop judging yourself so that you can live a life you love, free of weight drama."

— Julie

"Katy offers light and humor at the end of a long, dark tunnel we call 'DIET,' which should become a four-letter word ... "

— Charlotte

"Katy is real, honest, no-nonsense and also approachable and funny. You'll like yourself more after working with her."

— Lauree

"Katy is a fantastic coach! I highly recommend working with her to overcome the stress and anxiety of dieting. She really helped me change my mindset — even though I had convinced myself that I was focusing on a 'wellness lifestyle,' I was still tracking calories, negotiating with myself over what I should or shouldn't eat and getting angry at myself for cheating or going off plan. That's just exhausting and lead to constant feelings of failure. Working with Katy helped me reshape my thinking around food and exercise. Breaking the cycle with dieting doesn't mean giving up on yourself — once I shifted my mindset and took the pressure off, I actually started to lose some weight, enjoy my food more and enjoy working out."

— *Maureen*

"Katy is a fantastic coach. She is smart, gives great advice, is compassionate and understanding. She helps me set small manageable goals to work towards my larger goal. I feel like she can relate to my concerns and challenges and she celebrates my successes."

— *Daisy*

For more support beyond the book, visit **worthitwithkaty.com**.

ISBN Paperback: 978-0-692-95667-0

Printed in the United States of America

For Anna

Introduction:

My Story

Every Saturday morning for nearly five years, I went to a Weight Watchers meeting — first as a member, then as a lifetime member, and then as a leader.

Each week, I'd step on the scale. I'd remove my shoes, my jewelry, my watch. I'd make sure I hadn't eaten anything that morning. I would always empty my bladder. I wore the lightest clothes I could find (I weighed them at home ahead of time).

During the meetings, we would strategize how to get through family barbecues, or how to research menus online before going to restaurants. We would debate whether bananas really should be 0 points. We'd share tips, like using oil spray on roasted vegetables to keep the point value low, or drinking a big glass of water before a meal so you feel less hungry, or putting your fork down between bites to slow down your eating. We'd build imaginary sandwiches with the fewest points we could. We'd laugh. And cry. I'd hand out bravo stickers. We'd always leave feeling hopeful about our future.

We'd congratulate each other on our wins.

"I baked cookies for my daughter's class and didn't eat a single one!"
"For Valentine's Day, I told my husband to get me fruit instead of chocolates!"
"I lost this week, even though I ate a dessert 3 days ago!"

We'd commiserate.

"I don't know what's wrong. I did everything right this week, but I'm up today."
"Wait, when did a slice of pizza become 7 points?!"
"God, I miss french fries."

We'd confess our sins.

"I was making my son a peanut butter and jelly sandwich and I tasted a bit of peanut butter on my finger. Next thing I knew, I'd eaten half the jar!"
"After my weekly weigh-ins, I go out for a big splurge."

It was our church. Some of us came every week, and some came only during the holidays.

My husband once asked me what the meetings were like. I said, "Picture a cross between AA and Mary Kay."

• • •

So, how exactly does a Weight Watchers leader become an anti-diet crusader?

There was no magic flash of insight, no movie-worthy moment where mid-meeting I swept the fat-free snacks off the table, smashed the scales and threw open the meeting room door, raising my fist in the air.

In reality, the process was agonizingly slow and not exactly voluntary. There was lots of crying. And cursing. And hiding under the covers.

This is definitely not a weight loss book, so I'm sorry if that's what you were hoping for. This is also not a book that's going to give you any hard and fast answers, or frankly promise you anything.

Still with me? Great. This book is about me and my 28-year struggle with yo-yo dieting, binge eating and body shame. This book is about that pit of frustration and food obsession and body hatred that way too many of us are way too familiar with. This book is about how I fell into that pit, and how I finally began to crawl out. This book isn't about finding peace and freedom, but it is about looking for it.

• • •

I wasn't a fat kid. I wasn't skinny, either. I never had a

problem with my body. I wasn't picked on with that casual cruelty only children can really master. But I was tall. I always stood in the back row of my class pictures, which I thought sucked. But if you'd asked me then, I would have just said, "I'm average."

Until the 5th grade. My French teacher had the brilliant idea of teaching our class about kilograms by having each of us stand on a scale and calculate our weight ... IN FRONT OF THE WHOLE CLASS. And guess who weighed the most of all the girls? Yep. Right there, right then, in the most public of humiliations, I was irrevocably confirmed as "the heaviest girl." Even my 10-year-old brain instinctively knew that this was *the worst possible thing in the world*.

That day changed everything. From then on I would never again look at myself and not think about my size. There was something wrong with me. My body was unlovable. I should be ashamed.

At 14, puberty hit me like a freight train. My already "too large" body sprouted more horrifying curves. I went on my first official diet: Slim Fast. You never forget your first. Chalky brown shakes for breakfast and lunch, followed by a sensible dinner. It didn't last long, but it marked the beginning of the next 28 years of one diet or another. In my mind, my body had betrayed me and I had to do whatever I could to shrink.

I became a diet connoisseur. Low cal, low carb, no carb, low fat, high protein, high fat, low protein, gly-

KATY WEBER

cemic index, Atkins, South Beach, The Zone, Whole
30, paleo, French Women Don't Get Fat. I'd give
anything a shot. And each time, the results were
the same. Lose a few pounds. Hooray! Feel great,
lighten up a little, loosen the reins. Gain some back.
Shit. Gotta tighten the reins, gotta do better. Gotta
be better. Not coming off. Aw, fuck it. Give up. Eat
everything in sight. Gain back the weight. Gain back
more. Resume being a miserable diet failure.

At the age of 20, I stumbled onto my first dramatic
weight loss. It was the Fit for Life diet, created in the
1980s by California couple Harvey and Marilyn Di-
amond, and the rules were bizarre. Only fruit before
noon. After that, it was "all you could eat" vegetables. There were also limited carbs and proteins, but
you could *never eat them at the same time*. This basically meant I could choose between croutons and
cheese on my salads. I could handle that.

I lost so much weight that I got my first introduction
into the world of diet-related compliments.

"You look amazing!"
"How did you do it?!"
"So healthy!"
"You must feel great!"

Those compliments felt SO GOOD. But they also
came with the implicit understanding that a) I had
achieved something remarkable and was now deserving of envy and praise, and b) If I look amazing
NOW, guess how I didn't look before?

17

Well, that builds pressure. A lot of pressure. I'm amazing now, and I wasn't amazing before. Clearly, I need to stay amazing. I NEED TO STAY AMAZING. Pressure, of course, demands relief. And I found it in a new level of secret shame: binge eating.

I lived alone, so binging was easy. I was the picture of health in front of others, but alone? Up late, cramming for tests or furiously typing out essays at 4 a.m.? Easy. It started small. A little something. A reward for being good. For working hard. But it would snowball. I'd spin out. Stuffed. Uncomfortable. Depressed. Ashamed. I gained my Fit for Life weight back pretty quick. The compliments tapered off, and there I was, same old me, same old non-amazing self.

Eventually I picked myself up by the bootstraps and started a new diet. Every time it was the same. "I've got this," I'd say. "This one's for life! I'm making real, lasting changes.! I'm going to be thin! I'm going to look amazing! I'm going to BE amazing! I'd found the magic bullet! The secret to happines! I can't believe the rest of the world doesn't know about this." Yada yada. It was seductive.

The compliments would return, confirming for me yet again that I was only deserving of praise when I was actively losing weight.

Each diet was like a torrid love affair. They always began with passion and optimism. But then, the

18

bloom would fade. I'd relax and start to crave old habits — "bad foods," off menu, not on the plan. Then the internal struggle. I'd try so hard to be good and avoid the cravings, but instead I'd obsess over them. Then I'd promise, I'd SWEAR to myself, "It's just this once!" Get it out of my system. Get right back on track.

I was constantly trying not to fall off the wagon, clinging to it by my fingernails. But inevitably I'd fall off, and when I did, I'd fall hard. I'd fall with pleasure. With relief. Then came self-loathing. Guilt. Resignation. Depression.

"I have no will power."
"I gotta get my shit together."
"I'll start fresh Monday."

That was my 20s and early 30s. By the time I hit 36, I was resigned to a life of yo-yo dieting. Weight loss. Yay! Weight gain. Fuck. And I believed it was all my fault. I just lacked discipline. I had no self-control. C'est la vie.

I wasn't unhappy. I liked my life. I had a wonderful husband, 2 beautiful children, a decent career. But there was always a nagging belief that no matter how good things were, they'd be better if I lost weight. If I could just be thin, then I would REALLY be happy.

• • •

Enter Weight Watchers.

I had recently had my 2nd child, and my life felt overwhelming and out of control. It didn't help that my stubborn baby weight wasn't going anywhere. I ran into an old friend who'd lost an enormous amount of weight on the program. She was radiant. I was proud of her. She was proud of herself. I joined the very next day. I'd never paid for a weight loss program before, but I wanted what she had.

And I got it! It worked. Oh man, it worked! With my allotted daily points, I dropped pounds fast. I set a random goal weight for myself, smack dab in the middle of my "normal" BMI range, and I hit it in just 8 months. I had arrived. I had done it. I was finally thin. I was euphoric.

This wasn't a diet, I told myself. This was a lifestyle. This was MY lifestyle. I had finally learned the truth. This was the key to happiness. And now that I was in the club, I was never, ever, EVER going back! Sound familiar? ...

First, the good: There was the praise. I got noticed. Noticed by, like, everyone. The change was dramatic. There were ooohs. There were aaahs. I felt invincible. The compliments became such a constant fixture that if someone saw me and didn't immediately say, "You look amazing!", I'd wonder what the hell was wrong — either with them or with me.

I proudly posted "before and after" photos on Facebook. I evangelized the program, shouting from the rooftops: "Weight Watchers is amazing. I'm happier! A better mom! A better person!" I was reborn. I shed my former life, my former insecurities and, of course, all my former clothes.

I was also terrified. I'd been on this road before, and it always ended the same way. This time had to be different. So I became a Weight Watchers leader. I figured standing in front of members each week, not to mention the mandatory monthly weigh-ins, would have to keep me accountable.

But it was more than just accountability. I honestly felt the program was the greatest thing that had ever happened to me. I had earned the dream. I was finally thin! I was a superwoman! And I genuinely wanted to help others get there, too. I wanted to let them in on the secret, expand the club, help this group of desperate members reach their ultimate dream. I wouldn't — I couldn't! — let them down.

Well, it only took a month. Despite the weekly weigh-ins, obsessive point-counting, and preaching from the pulpit, the weight creep started. I could feel myself losing resolve. Same cycle. Same me. I'd be "good" for a day or two, maybe even three. Then I'd trip up. An indulgence. Then the regret and the chastising. And then the vow: I'll start fresh in the morning.

But the scoldings and the vows weren't enough. The magic was gone. My determination had flagged. My weight crept up. Restrict. Binge. Repeat.

Over those years, my eating grew more and more extreme. I'd wake with resolve and eat as little as possible throughout the day. Sometimes I'd skip dinner entirely, because in the back of my head I knew what was coming. I knew that at night, when the kids were asleep, I'd head to the kitchen and the flood gates would open. I'd eat thousands of calories, feeling completely incapable of stopping. So I increased my exercise. Gotta burn it off! Gotta make it up! Gotta keep this train on the tracks!

The nighttime eating only got worse. And more frequent. And each pound re-gained brought more stress. I was a failure. Everyone was so proud of me, and I was letting them down. I was letting myself down. Everyone must pity me now. And what about my members?! I'm such a hypocrite. I tout the program every Saturday, but I'm wildly off plan in my own life.

I was losing my hold on the new, amazing me. And as far as I was concerned, there was no bigger failure than returning to my old body.

Three years. For three years I slogged through this diet/binge cycle. Healthy, small portions while everyone was watching. Thousand-calorie mega binges every night. I was stressed, I was ashamed, I was miserable. And I was still gaining weight.

Then, on a New Year's Eve, I waited for my husband to go to bed and I rang in the new year with an epic binge to end all binges. After all, New Year's Day is the ultimate fresh start, right?

The next day, I woke up and immediately stepped on the scale to assess the damage. Horror. Shame. Vows. God, I was so tired of it all. I decided then that I had to cure myself of this binge eating once and for all. If I could just stop binge eating, I knew I would be thin again.

• • •

I started listening to podcasts, reading blogs, and researching as much as I could about binge eating and its root causes. Everything I came across pointed to the same conclusion: Your binge eating isn't the problem, it's a symptom of another problem. Dieting.

Oh crap. You can't be serious. If I really want to end binge eating, I have to stop dieting? How the hell am I supposed to stop dieting? And how the hell am I going to lose weight if I'm not dieting?

Where did this notion come from? It's left out of diet literature. Weight Watchers never even hinted at it. After decades of restricting and binge eating, this was the very first time it had ever occurred to me that restrictive eating habits might be the cause of out-of-control eating. I had never made this connection before. No adult ever suggested this to me when I was growing up. No physician had ever mentioned this. This was completely novel information to me, and it was pretty shattering.

This was definitely NOT the answer I wanted. This did not fit into my plan. I did not want to believe it.

But I also knew it made perfect sense. If I wanted to cure myself of binge eating, I needed to stop restricting my food. I needed to feed myself enough that I wouldn't need to overcompensate with binges.

I was terrified. Eat whatever I want? Surely I'd gain a ton of weight. It felt wrong. It felt like giving up. It felt chaotic and irresponsible. It felt *unhealthy*.

So I conjured up a foolproof plan. I'd eat as much as I wanted, but I'd limit the types of food I ate. I figured I could feed myself AND lose weight if I only ate non-processed, grass-fed, organic, pasture-raised, sprouted grain, sanctimonious, morally superior food. Sugar became Satan.

And it worked! Well, sorta. I had a few good months. Things were looking up, binge eating was under control, weight went down. But it didn't last. It couldn't last. Why? *Because I was still restricting my food.* Sure, it wasn't the amount this time, but restriction is restriction. And every meal, every choice, every non-GMO, locally sourced, hand-picked leaf of kale I cooked had the same old underlying motivation. Weight loss. Weight loss. Weight loss. And soon the binges came back. The cycle reset.

24

• • •

One evening, as I sat at dinner with my family and I was the only one eating my grass-fed burger without a bun, I looked over at my 8-year-old daughter. Man, I love this girl. When I look at her, I'm so proud of her. And I think, When she looks at me, what does she see? She sees my sad bunless burger. She sees mommy eats differently than she and the boys. What message am I sending her? Am I teaching her about health? Am I teaching her about self-care? About confidence? Or am I teaching her what I'd learned, whether I meant to or not: that thinness is the goal above all else. You have to fight for it at all costs. And you have to fight for it every day, forever.

Did I really want this path for her — a lifetime of dieting and feeling like her body wasn't good enough? That she wasn't good enough? Did I want her to obsess about thinness, to believe weight loss would make her happier when I knew this wasn't the case? Did I want her to feel somehow deficient if she was taller and larger than her friends? Did I want her to spend even a fraction of a minute longing to be anything other than her perfect self? No. No. No. A thousand times no.

I was done. Done weighing my portions. Done politely declining things I loved. Done feeling constantly anxious around food and forever fearing the next binge. It was just too much. I knew what I wanted for my daughter. It was easy. Food and body freedom. So how come I couldn't want that for my-self? Turns out I could. Turns out I did.

• • •

When you've spent your whole life obsessing about what you eat, it is very, VERY hard to intentionally stop. But I did it. All foods were allowed. Nothing was off the table. Seconds? Sure. Snack? Why not? I ate when I felt like it. I indulged my cravings. I listened to my hunger. I felt like I was cheating.

This was all wildly new to me. Yes, I felt like I'd broken out of my chains, but I also felt like I'd given up on myself. A nagging voice told me, "A dream has died. A better version of you *has died.*" Because for me, self-care was always synonymous with weight loss. And if I give up on one, I would clearly be giving up on the other.

I quit Weight Watchers. I quit restricting. I started to really eat. I put aside my fear of weight gain and gave myself permission to enjoy. Enjoy myself. Enjoy food. Enjoy my body, at any size.

It was crazy at first. I ate everything in sight. I fed every craving. I ate lots of ice cream and chocolate. I ate burgers (with buns) and fries. I'd been restricting myself for 28 years, and dammit I was hungry! Did I gain weight? Most definitely. I had to. My clothes got tight. I felt huge. I cried. A lot. But I knew what I needed, and I made it through.

That was hard. I feared I was making a huge mistake. But I pushed on, not because I knew what I was doing was right, but because anything else seemed wrong.

Slowly, something magical started to happen. I was changing. I was tuning in. I was understanding my body's hunger cues for the first time since, well, ever. And soon I stopped eating everything in sight. Endless ice cream can actually become tedious. Who knew, right? And chocolate? Even beautiful, luxurious, near-perfect chocolate can lose its appeal when you know it's available anytime you want it. The pendulum, which had swung furiously in both directions for so many years, had started to settle. And I felt it — a stillness, a peace. I had stopped restricting. I had stopped binging. I was free.

• • •

Diets have a basic promise. Lose weight. Feel great. Get congratulated. Get complimented. You've done a good job. You're a good person. Your confidence soars.

But nobody talks about what comes next. How our bodies fight back. How maintaining is harder than losing. How you start to feel betrayed. What's wrong with me? I'm trying so hard to be good and yet I'm a failure. I have no will power. I'm a disgrace.

The weight slowly comes back. The compliments cease, and their silence is even louder. You hear the judgment in the quiet. "So sad for her." "She couldn't keep it up." "She gave up." "She looks terrible." "She must be so unhealthy." It's pain. It's shame. Your confidence is in the toilet.

So, new vows. New diets. Yada yada. Rinse. Repeat.

It's exhausting. It's demoralizing. But it's also comfortable. It's all we know. It may be a vicious cycle, but we don't know what else to do. Leaping off that cliff? Now, that's truly terrifying. Terrifying and lonely, and every second is a second of self-doubt.

Dieting is an addiction. And breaking any addiction takes guts beyond measure. It was hard to face my inner critic. It was hard to silence that voice shouting "Get your act together!" and "Get the body you've always wanted, the body you've always deserved."

I still have doubts. Diet culture is a hurricane that swirls around every aspect of modern life — in schools, at work, at the supermarket, on television, in movies, at the gym. I constantly feel the pull. Do I have what it takes to withstand it? There are days I simply can't, and so I stay home and cry. There are people I avoid because I hear their thoughts, and their thoughts are not kind. A part of me cries out over and over, "STOP THIS. YOU ARE MAKING A HUGE MISTAKE. GO BACK TO WHERE IT'S SAFE." Sometimes I wonder if I'll ever feel proud of my body again.

But then, my daughter.

I imagine saying to her all the things I so easily say to myself. I imagine her thinking she's not enough just as she is. I wonder how long till she doubts her own self-worth? Till she feels envious of the thinnest girl in the room. I wonder if it's already too late.

She needs to know she's perfect as she is. She doesn't need to change. She is loved. She is accepted. She is enough. And that belief must start with me. I will be brave for her.

I think back to my younger self. Adolescent me, fighting my body. Wanting to be thin. Wanting to be accepted.

But that acceptance I craved? It wasn't from others. It was from myself. I know that now. I never accepted myself. I never gave myself a chance. That ends now, too. I'm saying no. No to the voices, the demons, the self-loathing. The shame. I'm untangling a lifetime of negative self-image and self-criticism. I'm saying no to fear, and I'm moving forward the only way I know how.

• • •

So, let's get to it. The chapters that follow are divided into six themes. Each was an essential step for me in my own recovery from the diet-binge cycle and my quest for food and body freedom.

I wrote this book for me. I wanted to remind myself of how far I've come, and how there's no turning back. I don't always know if I'm doing the right thing, but for now doing anything else feels wrong. I've chosen to put my trust in that gut feeling, simply because I'm out of options and I need to keep going.

I wrote this book for you, wherever you are on your journey. It's slow and it's hard. It's really hard. And if you feel scared and frustrated, know that you're not alone. You'll get through this.

And I wrote this book for our daughters. When I look at them and think of their future and all that they will accomplish regardless of the size of their bodies, I know that this journey is worth it.

Step 1:

Ditch the Diets

Dieting:
(di•et•ing - verb; used with object)

Doing the same thing over and over and
expecting different results.
(see also: stu•pid•ity)

• • •

What do I mean when I talk about dieting?

Dieting is any form of restrictive eating done specifically to control and alter your body's size. Counting calories, avoiding certain food groups, eating like a caveman, portion control — if it's done to lose weight, then it's dieting.

What's so wrong with dieting?

Imagine a company sells you a product with a 95 percent failure rate. Then, the company blames you when the product doesn't work, claiming you're just not using it right, or you just don't have the will power or self-control to use it correctly.

And then they claim the only way to fix the product is to buy more of it. Sounds ridiculous, right?

Possibly criminal? Well, guess what. That's the diet industry.

• • •

We've all heard the statistic that 95 percent of diets fail, meaning the dieters gain back all the weight within 2 to 5 years. Why is this? It can't be that 95 percent of us are just lazy and lacking the will power to stick with the diet regimen. Yet that's what we dieters believe, and it's why we keep going back over and over, thinking, "This time I'll get it right and I won't screw up."

But what if it's not our fault at all? What if the inevitable weight gain isn't because we've given up on ourselves or we're doing the diet wrong? What if it's actually a sign that our bodies are healthy and doing everything right?

From birth, a body's weight is determined by genetics. Like height or skin color or shoe size, each body has an ideal weight called our set point weight. This weight is the point at which our metabolism is most stable, and at which our body operates at its optimal health.

I first heard about this mysterious set point weight when I read *Health at Every Size: The Surprising Truth About Your Weight*, a groundbreaking book by researcher Linda Bacon that describes the biology behind how our bodies react to dieting.

As Bacon explains, while you might believe your set point weight should be MUCH lower than your current weight, your body might not agree with you. Sure, it feels great when you go on a diet and start to lose weight, but your body enters a state of alarm. It starts to suspect something is wrong — "Wait, what's happened to all the food?!" — and it begins to protect you from starvation. While your conscious mind knows that you're not starving, your biological self has no idea.

When you lose weight, your body's full-time job becomes gaining that weight back by any means necessary. The body loves homeostasis (maintaining a constant balance), and it fights hard to maintain it.[1]

Here's what happens next: When your body thinks you are starving, the *hypothalamus*, which is the part of your brain that controls your hunger and fullness cues, increases the production of *ghrelin*, the hormone that signals hunger, and it begins to reduce production of *leptin*, the hormone that signals you are full.[2]

So when you're starving, your body increases your appetite to get you to eat more, and reduces your fullness cues to store up more food than you need (in case you're ever found to be starving again).

This is why we so often binge on fatty or sugary foods when dieting. Our brains actually make those foods — the ones that will provide the most energy in the quickest amount of time — the most appealing, and eventually we dive into them with urgent desperation.

Meanwhile, to make the most of the reduced energy from your limited food intake, your metabolism slows and your desire for activity decreases in an effort to try to keep your weight stable (think of it like a thermostat).[3]

The less you eat, the harder your body works to make the most of the food you consume in order to get you back to your set point weight. You fixate on food. (Have you ever noticed how much time you spend researching recipes and planning your next meal when you're dieting? That's not a coincidence.)

When you're dieting, you're basically declaring war on your body.

This is why maintaining weight loss is so difficult. Eventually we get more efficient at holding onto weight, even with fewer calories.[4] And dieting can also backfire by resetting your set point weight at a higher level in order to protect you against future diets. This is why we gain more weight than when we started dieting. Each time we diet, we store extra fat, even after the dieting ends. *In fact, dieting is consistently listed as the number one predictor of future weight gain.*[5]

With each new diet, we lose less weight than before, and "fall off the wagon" even faster. I've met many Weight Watchers members who'd return time and time again, claiming, "This is the only program that works for me." And I would desperately want to say, "But clearly it's not working if you have to come back over and over!"

When diets fail, we tell ourselves it's because we've stopped trying, we've lost will power, we're just not working hard enough. But it's actually because our bodies are working hard at trying to save us — they've become very efficient at trying to stop the weight loss in order to keep us at our set point weight so we can perform at our optimal health.

Why do so many of us binge when dieting?

"For every diet, there is an equal and opposite binge." — Geneen Roth

In my own experience, binge eating as I experienced it ranged from guiltily stuffing brownies in my mouth at a party, to going back to my cupboard for that fourth or fifth helping of cookies no matter how hard I'd try to hide them way in the back. Or I'd have a few too many glasses of wine and say "screw it" and eat an entire pint of Ben & Jerry's.

In all its forms, it was a tightly-wound feeling of being out of control. It was food was calling to me and me being powerless to resist. It was eating quickly and beyond fullness, always tinged with guilt and shame.

No matter what, I'd go to bed feeling stuffed and disgusted with myself. I'd vow this was the last time I'd ever do it, and I'd start fresh with the diet in the morning.

Sound familiar?

Binge eating is not just a lack of will power, or laziness, or an uncontrollable love of cookies. Binge eating is the direct result of restrictive eating. The longer you stay in a state of starvation, the more likely you are to feast when the opportunity arises. We are wired to overcompensate whenever we under-eat.[6] The only way to end the binge eating is to end the restrictive eating.

If I don't diet, then how else am I supposed to lose weight?

If dieting is how we lose weight, but dieting is harmful and actually makes us gain weight in the long run, then what are we supposed to do if we want to lose weight?

For starters, evaluate *why* you want to lose weight in the first place. Did your doctor tell you to do it for your health? Are you uncomfortable with your body? Do you feel like your life would be better? Is there actually anything wrong with your health, or are you just larger than you'd like?

When it comes to weight loss, dieting is the only

method most of us have ever known. Our friends and family are always dieting. Our doctors tell us to diet, and our culture and media drown us in the message day in and day out. Our obsession with weight loss is so commonplace that we've never really thought to question it.

Whenever we've tried losing weight, we initially see results. Any diet, no matter how absurd, usually results in weight loss. But when the weight comes back, we never blame the diet. Instead, we blame ourselves for our lack of will power and our inability to stick with it.

You can't blame us for wanting to lose weight. We're besieged from birth with messages that thin is beautiful and healthy, that thinner people are happier people. Hell, they most likely are, but that's not because of their weight. It's because they're accepted and praised in our society.

It also has nothing to do with their superior health. In fact, several studies have shown that people with BMI (body mass index) ranges in the "overweight" category tend to live longer than their "normal" weight counterparts.[7]

Slightly heavier people are also more likely to survive heart attacks and other serious illnesses, and elderly people who were overweight lived longer than those of a "healthy weight."[8]

So, if you are dieting because your ultimate goal is

to be healthy, reduce pain and to have more energy and self-confidence, you can do all of these things without having to focus exclusively on weight loss.

We've been taught to believe that weight loss is integral to health and happiness. In fact, the multi-billion dollar weight loss industry thrives on the ongoing belief that the less you weigh, the happier you'll be.

But it's also an industry that thrives because their products don't work. When Oprah Winfrey first announced she was buying a 10 percent stake in Weight Watchers, *New York Magazine* called it a "brilliant investment," but not for the reason you'd think.

"It's brilliant not because Weight Watchers works but because it doesn't. It's the perfect business model. People give Weight Watchers the credit when they lose weight. Then they regain the weight and blame themselves. This sets them up to join Weight Watchers all over again, and they do."[9]

But my doctor told me I have to lose weight

Pre-diabetic? High blood pressure? High cholesterol? Whatever the reason, your doctor has told you in no uncertain terms: You need to lose weight. Maybe you've been told this so many times that you avoid going to the doctor, dreading the inevitable judgment.

So what do you do? Well, for starters, remember that there are no diseases that are caused by fat. There is no such thing as a disease that only fat people have. Sure, we've all heard the statistics that obesity puts you at an increased risk of heart disease, high cholesterol, and diabetes. But this is merely a correlative relationship, not a causal relationship.

In other words, the habits, genetics, and countless other factors that are causing the obesity are also causing the disease. Fix the habits and other factors, and you have a better chance of curing the disease. If doctors told us this (instead of simply saying, "Lose weight"), it would be a lot easier to focus on our health instead of the scale.

Changing lifestyle habits is a much better way to reduce your risk of disease. For instance, eating more fruits and vegetables is a healthy lifestyle change, as is regular physical movement and exercise. But an equally healthy lifestyle change might be getting more rest, getting out of a destructive relationship, or finding a more satisfying career.

• • •

In *Health at Every Size*, Bacon recounts her 2006 study at the U.S. Department of Agriculture in which her team recruited participants by advertising for "large women who were struggling with their weight and interested in feeling better about themselves and improving their health." The women were placed into either the Health at Every Size® program or a traditional weight-loss program. Women in the weight-loss program were instructed to eat less, count calories, and exercise more.

Bacon recalls that the Health at Every Size® group were encouraged to eat when they were hungry and to appreciate the feeling of fullness, to make healthy food choices, and to find a style of physical activity that was most enjoyable for them. They were also given techniques to build their self-esteem and to increase the confidence they had in their bodies. While they were deeply disappointed that they were not in the weight-loss group, they stuck it out. In fact, the HAES® group had a higher retention rate than the dieting group.

The HAES® participants were taught about the science behind weight loss, why some bodies naturally weigh more than others, why conventional recommendations to diet or exercise may not have much impact on weight in the long run, and why weight is not an important factor in measuring one's health or worth.

The dieting group dieted.

In the end, the women participating in the HAES® program didn't lose weight, but they emerged with higher self-esteem, a healthier relationship with food, and better physical health. The dieters experienced none of these benefits, and while they did initially lose weight, *all of them* gained it back.

After two years, both groups weighed approximately the same as before the study, but the women in the HAES® group had healthier blood pressure, lower cholesterol, and they were more physically active than the dieting group. (I'll get back to the Health at Every Size® movement in Step 3.)

So the next time your doctor tells you to lose weight as a solution to your medical problems, ask, "What would you say to a thin person with the same disease or symptoms?"

If I'm not dieting, aren't I just giving up?

Even if I'm not successful at keeping the weight off, at least I'm trying, right?

Let's get this straight: the pursuit of weight loss rarely produces the thin, happy life we've dreamt of for any significant length of time. Not only is the weight loss fleeting, but when the weight comes back, we feel like bigger failures than before. The emotional damage alone is enough to stop dieting, but many of us feel like if we stop, we're somehow "giving up" on this healthier, happier version of ourselves.

When I read *Health at Every Size* and realized my constant yo-yo dieting was leading to weight gain and poor health, I was devastated. On the one hand, I knew I didn't want to diet anymore, but on the other hand, I still wanted to lose weight! My entire notion of self-care was defined by dieting, exercise and the constant pursuit of weight loss.

I wanted to be healthy, but I wasn't ready to let go of the dream of a naturally, effortless thin body. I was also afraid to simply eat whatever I wanted. I can't trust myself, I thought. If left to my own devices, I knew I'd overeat and likely balloon into a whale! I needed rules, guidelines, calorie counts from whichever book, magazine article or weight loss program could tell me "the right way to eat."

But that fear — where I was convinced I'd eat everything and anything in sight — was the direct result of years of dieting. When we're told over and over that we aren't eating properly and we have no self-control around food, we believe it. And when we give away that control and follow diet rules, we lose our innate ability to monitor our own hunger and fullness.

Dieting makes "cheating" inevitable. You don't trust yourself around certain foods, so you go hog wild whenever they're around. But trusting yourself can be re-learned once you start to tune out the diet talk and tune in to what your body is telling you it needs.

You can start making choices because you want to, not because you think you should, which means you'll be more likely to maintain them in the long run. You'll be approaching your health with positivity, instead of fear and self-criticism. Dropping the pursuit of weight loss isn't about giving up, it's about being free.

If your health is really your priority, then remember this: Dieting is not "healthier" than non-dieting. "Simply trying" is not healthier than letting go. Yo-yo dieting hurts your metabolism, your energy levels, and the way your body processes food. And it isn't healthier than staying overweight. People with stable weights, even higher ones, tend to have better health than yo-yo dieters.[10]

Ditching dieting doesn't mean you're a failure. Instead, it means you're walking away from a method that doesn't work, doesn't promote health, and actually causes your body to gain weight over time. Ditching dieting means ending a war you were destined to lose.

It may sound scary, but once you allow ALL foods and start listening to your body again, you'll find your way and regulate your intake. Take the leap of faith and end the dieting mentality today.

While you're at it, ditch the scale

Seriously. Throw it out. It's not serving you.

"But without my scale, I'll never know my weight!"
Yes, that's the point.
"But if I stop weighing myself, I'm afraid I'll let myself go."
Exactly.

There are so many other factors besides a number on the scale that contribute to overall health and wellness, such as regular exercise, reducing your stress levels, getting adequate sleep, eating a variety of foods, and proper self-care.

That little number staring back at us has such an enormous impact on how we feel and the choices we make. Since any effort to reduce that number proves counterproductive for the overwhelming majority of us, it's best to simply eliminate it from your vocabulary.

By ditching the scale, you're recognizing that this number is meaningless when it comes to your health and your worth. You are more than that number. If weighing yourself is dictating how you feel about your body, it's time to stop.

OK fine, dieting isn't worth it. But now what?!

So, what's the solution? Once I was able to shift my focus away from food restriction and forced weight loss, I moved toward relaxed eating and living. I began to trust my hunger cues and my cravings again. In the next chapter, I discuss the concept of intuitive eating and how following my gut and learning to eat intuitively was key to my journey to food and body freedom.

Step 2:

Follow Your Gut

OK, fine. Let's say I stop trying to lose weight. But what's the difference between dieting and simply eating healthy? I mean, we're supposed to eat healthy, right? And eating healthy means I'll lose weight, right?

Yes and no. You might, you might not. The point is: It doesn't matter, because ultimately you are not in control of your body's functions. Your job is to help your body out by listening to your gut, and following your intuition about what you feel like eating, not what you think you should eat.

What exactly is healthy eating?

There are plenty of books out there that will tell you all the different types of healthy foods and what you should eat and what you should avoid, but this isn't one of them.

We all know the basics: Eat more fruit, vegetables, whole grains, beans, legumes. But after that, it gets murky. Carbs or no carbs? Gluten, yay or nay? Dairy? Eating like a caveman? Wait, are we putting coconut oil in our coffee now?

Healthy eating, above all, is pleasurable. This means being able to give some thought to your food selection so you get nutritious food, but not being so rigid or restrictive that you miss out on enjoyable food. In fact, studies have shown that experiencing pleasure when eating increases your metabolism and absorption of nutrients, while the opposite occurs when eating with feelings of guilt and regret.[11]

Healthy eating is flexible. This means giving yourself permission to eat sometimes because you are happy, sad, bored, or just because it feels good.

Healthy eating is intuitive. Listen to your hunger cues and trust that your body will crave what you need, when you need it.

Healthy eating means feeding yourself. Eat whenever you're hungry and stop when you're satisfied. The more you restrict your body's own natural desire for food, the more likely you are to overcompensate and feel "out of control" with food later on. Make sure you are always satisfied with the delicious, nutritious foods that you love.

Eat your damn burger with a bun.

What is not healthy eating?

Eating something because you think it will help you lose weight is not healthy eating. As soon as you stop listening to your own body's hunger and start counting calories or points or macros, you are more likely to start the cycle of restriction/overcompensation. Don't be ruled by lists of "food to eat" and "food to avoid."

Take, for example, fat-free foods. Fat can be scary to the chronic dieter, but your body needs healthy fats. Dietary fats are essential to give your body energy and to support cell growth. They help protect your organs and keep your body temperature stable. Fats also help your body absorb nutrients and produce important hormones.

Every time you try to avoid fat by purchasing a "fat-free" or "light" product, you are depriving your body of real fat and replacing it with artificial sugars, chemicals, and additives put there to enhance the flavor lost by the fat. They're not natural. Your body doesn't know what to do with them, and it can't burn them efficiently.

That said, banning certain foods or food groups because you think they're bad for you is also not healthy eating. The more you label foods "good" or "bad," the more likely you are to crave the "bad" and feel out of control around those foods. Stress around food isn't healthy. Give yourself permission to eat all foods, and enjoy variety. You'll figure out what you like or don't like.

Skipping meals or eating on the run is not healthy eating. Take the time to sit down, slow down, tune in and enjoy your food. You're more likely to stop when full, and less likely to overeat.[12]

Listen to your body

Once all food was on the table, I was able to take the time to discover what foods made my body *feel* good.

I asked myself: Is this meal delicious? Will this fill me up? Will this nourish me? How will I feel about myself after I've eaten it? Will I feel satisfied? Will I feel deprived? Will I feel happy or will I feel depressed after eating it?

How does a salad for lunch make me feel? How does a bag of Cheetos make me feel? What about a cheeseburger and fries? How does it feel when I haven't had any water all day? What foods give me energy? What makes me feel sluggish? What am I truly craving right now?

Your body gives you feedback all the time — it's up to you to start tuning in. A great experiment for this is to take a dozen of your favorite cookies and practice intuitive eating.

Rather than immediately seizing up with fear over

the fact that you might eat them all, approach them with delight. How does that first one taste? What about the second one? And the third one? Keep noticing how each cookie tastes compared to the previous one. After a while, that initial feeling of mouth-watering pleasure goes away.

So, what leads us to go beyond that point and stuff them all in our mouth? For one thing, it's guilt. Maybe we're disgusted with ourselves and we want to get rid of the evidence. Maybe we tell ourselves this is a one-time cheat, so we want as many as possible. Whatever it is, it's a backlash against the judgment you had about yourself for eating a cookie in the first place. Your carefully maintained willpower around food has just been tampered with, and naturally you feel like all hell just broke loose.

But when the guilt and judgment is taken away, it's possible to decide for yourself how many cookies you actually want. Maybe it's one cookie, maybe it's more. The point is, there's no wrong way to eat them. You can eat what you want, when you want, and your body will let you know how you're doing. In time, it becomes very hard to eat a dozen cookies when you're no longer guiltily eating them as fast as possible.

What is "intuitive eating"?

Registered dietitian Evelyn Tribole and nutrition therapist Elyse Resch first coined the phrase in their

1995 book, *Intuitive Eating*. Intuitive eating is a basic nutritional philosophy that rejects dieting, restriction and food rules in exchange for listening to your body's innate biological wisdom. You listen to your body's hunger and fullness cues, learn to trust yourself to make decisions around what or how much to eat, and rebuild self-trust around eating those "forbidden" foods.

We are all born intuitive eaters. Haven't you ever marveled at a young child's ability to eat half a cupcake and then announce he's done? He's not worried about how that cupcake will sabotage his diet. He doesn't vow that this is the last time he'll ever have a cupcake. He enjoys it until he's done, whenever that is. That's intuitive eating.

Children naturally know when they're full. They graze, they snack, they eat next to nothing one day and then inhale everything the next day. As parents, we tend to worry about their nutritional needs, but research has shown that when young children are given the freedom to choose when and what they want to eat from a wide variety of foods, they instinctively choose food that offer an appropriate nutritional balance.[13]

As children grow, and the more we grown ups interfere, they lose this ability. We teach them to sit for 3 meals a day and limit snacks in between, to eat their vegetables if they want dessert. We praise them when they clean their plate. We teach them how to stop listening to their bodies and how to start adhering to external rules about when, what and how much to eat. We see their pudgy little bodies and wonder if we're feeding them too much. Or we see their skinny bodies and worry that we're not feeding them enough.

A study by registered dietitian and renowned family feeding expert Ellyn Satter showed pressuring children to eat "healthy foods" actually makes them want to eat them less, and restricted eating in general can lead children to overcompensate and eat even when they're not hungry.[14]

The very first time we're put on a diet, whether it was of our own volition or we were put on one by a parent or a doctor, we buy into the idea that somehow our body has let us down and it can't be trusted to do its job properly. It's a big fat slap in the face to our body's intuition. By dieting, we're saying, "I no longer believe that my body can make its own decisions about eating." So instead we follow an external set of rules, a certain prescribed amount of calories, or some fad diet we read about online. Regardless of the source or the principles, we are exchanging our natural instincts for a rigid idea of how we should eat.

The only time I remember being an intuitive eater during my dieting days was when I was pregnant. It was the one time in my life that I wasn't worried about weight gain, and as a result, I could really listen to my cravings, no matter how weird they were. With my first pregnancy, all I wanted was mac 'n' cheese (something I normally can't stand) and French fries (ok, that's never changed). For a long time, I couldn't even bring vegetables anywhere near my mouth without gagging. With my second pregnancy, I couldn't seem to eat enough clementines.

During those nine month periods, I allowed my body to be in charge. It was the only time I felt free and happy around food. However, the minute those babies popped out, I went back to worrying about my weight and restricting my food.

• • •

In their book, Tribole and Resch came up with "10 Principles of Intuitive Eating," which can also be found on their website. I've reprinted them here:

1. **Reject the Diet Mentality.** Throw out the diet books and magazine articles that offer you false hope of losing weight quickly, easily, and permanently. Get angry at the lies that have led you to feel as if you were a failure every time a new diet stopped working and you gained back all of the weight. If you allow even one small hope to linger that a new and better diet might be lurking around the corner, it will prevent you from being free to rediscover Intuitive Eating.

2. **Honor Your Hunger.** Keep your body biologically fed with adequate energy and carbohydrates. Otherwise you can trigger a primal drive to overeat. Once you reach the moment of excessive hunger, all intentions of moderate, conscious eating are fleeting and

irrelevant. Learning to honor this first biological sig-
nal sets the stage for re-building trust with yourself
and food.

3. **Make Peace with Food.** Call a truce, stop the food
fight! Give yourself unconditional permission to eat.
If you tell yourself that you can't or shouldn't have
a particular food, it can lead to intense feelings of
deprivation that build into uncontrollable cravings
and, often, bingeing. When you finally "give-in"
to your forbidden food, eating will be experienced
with such intensity, it usually results in Last Supper
overeating, and overwhelming guilt.

4. **Challenge the Food Police.** Scream a loud "NO"
to thoughts in your head that declare you're "good"
for eating minimal calories or "bad" because you ate
a piece of chocolate cake. The Food Police monitor
the unreasonable rules that dieting has created. The
police station is housed deep in your psyche, and
its loud speaker shouts negative barbs, hopeless
phrases, and guilt-provoking indictments. Chasing
the Food Police away is a critical step in returning to
Intuitive Eating.

5. **Respect Your Fullness.** Listen for the body signals
that tell you that you are no longer hungry. Observe
the signs that show that you're comfortably full.
Pause in the middle of a meal or food and ask yourself how the food tastes, and what is your current
fullness level?

6. **Discover the Satisfaction Factor.** The Japanese

have the wisdom to promote pleasure as one of their goals of healthy living In our fury to be thin and healthy, we often overlook one of the most basic gifts of existence–the pleasure and satisfaction that can be found in the eating experience. When you eat what you really want, in an environment that is inviting and conducive, the pleasure you derive will be a powerful force in helping you feel satisfied and content. By providing this experience for yourself, you will find that it takes much less food to decide you've had "enough".

7. **Honor Your Feelings Without Using Food.** Find ways to comfort, nurture, distract, and resolve your issues without using food. Anxiety, loneliness, boredom, anger are emotions we all experience throughout life. Each has its own trigger, and each has its own appeasement. Food won't fix any of these feelings. It may comfort for the short term, distract from the pain, or even numb you into a food hangover. But food won't solve the problem. If anything, eating for an emotional hunger will only make you feel worse in the long run. You'll ultimately have to deal with the source of the emotion, as well as the discomfort of overeating.

8. **Respect Your Body.** Accept your genetic blueprint. Just as a person with a shoe size of eight would not expect to realistically squeeze into a size six, it is equally as futile (and uncomfortable) to have the same expectation with body size. But mostly, respect your body, so you can feel better about who you are. It's hard to reject the diet mentality if you are unreal-

istic and overly critical about your body shape.

9. **Exercise – Feel the Difference.** Forget militant exercise. Just get active and feel the difference. Shift your focus to how it feels to move your body, rather than the calorie burning effect of exercise. If you focus on how you feel from working out, such as energized, it can make the difference between rolling out of bed for a brisk morning walk or hitting the snooze alarm. If when you wake up, your only goal is to lose weight, it's usually not a motivating factor in that moment of time.

10. **Honor Your Health – Gentle Nutrition.** Make food choices that honor your health and tastebuds while making you feel well. Remember that you don't have to eat a perfect diet to be healthy. You will not suddenly get a nutrient deficiency or gain weight from one snack, one meal, or one day of eating. It's what you eat consistently over time that matters, progress not perfection is what counts.[15]

• • •

Trust your body

If I allow myself to simply eat anything I want, I will eat everything in sight!

What is your reaction when I say, "Eat whatever you want, whenever you want"? Does it bring up a feeling of freedom and excitement? Or does it strike fear that you'll end up eating endless amounts of junk food on the couch and gaining 300 pounds overnight?

If it's the latter, then you fear overeating (likely because you've done it many times in the past). This fear of overeating when you "let loose on food" is the result of a dieter's mentality, a deeply ingrained belief that we can't be trusted around food and therefore we need to be told what and how much to eat.

But just as we've lost our intuitive abilities through years of dieting, frustration, restricting and binge eating, we can re-learn intuitive eating over time.

The first step is to stop "shoulding" all over yourself and trust the process. Allow all food and eat to your heart's content. Sound scary? Remember, your guilt and fear associated with food is exactly what is leading to your overeating in the first place. The only way to overcome this for good is to stop feeling guilty and afraid, and make all foods available to you.

I often like to tell my clients to pick one "fear food" — something they can't have in the house because they just know they'll eat the whole thing. Maybe it's chocolate chips, or maybe it's Oreos or peanut butter or ice cream or Doritos. Whatever it is, go out and buy it. Have it in the house. Give yourself unrestricted permission to eat it.

You might eat the whole bag the first night. If you do, that's OK. Just go out and buy another one. Maybe you'll eat that, too. Go out and buy another one. Keep repeating this and you'll quickly find that it will lose its hold on you. Eventually you will stop. Your body will say enough is enough. And when that happens, you'll have successfully tuned in to your body's needs, and the fear of that food will have disappeared.

I stole this idea from Geneen Roth, the best-selling author who has written extensively about compulsive eating and dieting. In her article "Kindness and calories," she writes about a client whose 11-year-old daughter was hiding food from her. The mother was vigilant about the girl's food at mealtime, but the girl was still gaining weight.

Roth suggested that the mother fill up a pillowcase with M&M's and give it to her daughter. Whenever it would get a quarter empty, she was to fill it back up. She told her to come back in a month and tell her how it went.

The mother came back and reported that initially her daughter took the pillowcase everywhere, even to bed. During the second week, she stopped taking the pillowcase to school. She ate fewer M&M's.

By the third week, she hardly touched them. By week four, she never wanted to see another M&M again.

When we make food fully available to us, and when we stop fearing that it won't be there tomorrow or that something terrible will happen if we eat it, we eventually lose the tendency to overindulge and it quickly loses its hold over us.

As Roth says later in the same article: "Most people say they gain weight when they eat what they want. But the truth is that people gain weight when they eat what they don't want — and then eat copious amounts of what they do want because they're afraid they'll be deprived again. They gain weight because they argue with themselves constantly and then, bruised from the argument, eat ice cream to be kind to themselves."[16]

• • •

Your body is smart — it tells you when to stop eating, as long as you're paying attention. In fact, food actually becomes less desirable to your brain when you aren't hungry anymore.[17] This is called "alliesthesia." You know how a hot shower feels great when you're cold but feels stifling when you're already overheated? That's alliesthesia. The enjoyment of an external stimulus depends on your internal state. When you're really hungry, a bite of food is delicious. But after the first few bites, when you're beginning to feel satisfied, your taste receptors actually begin to weaken, sending a message to your taste buds that you're losing interest in the food. (Remember the experiment with the 12 cookies?)

Intuitive eaters are more likely than dieters to maintain a healthy body weight, and they're more likely to feel happier about their bodies.[18] Paying close attention to how your food choices affect your physical well-being will eventually lead to a more well-balanced, nutritious approach to eating. And once you aren't afraid of food or eating, non-desirable food won't need to be quickly shoved into your mouth for fear you'll never get it again.

Our society's ongoing assumption is that people are overweight because they eat more, and they just need to eat smaller portions in order to successfully lose weight. But this isn't actually the case. In fact, several U.S. studies have found that higher weight people eat no more than thinner people.[19]

It's only when the body is being underfed that it begins to overcompensate by reducing your metabolism, storing all extra calories as fat, and making you crave and obsess over certain foods.[20] When you reduce your portions, you increase the likelihood of binge eating and re-gaining any weight that was initially lost.

Almost always, the answer is to eat *more*, not less.

• • •

Intuitive eating can be really scary to embrace at first, especially if you feel like you have a lot of weight to lose. After so many years of desperately trying to lose weight, eating without limits felt downright terrifying to me. I kept thinking, *I shouldn't be eating this*. But I trusted the process and kept dismissing the "shouldn't" voice. In time, I learned to understand what my cravings were and what my limits were, too.

It turns out I still love salads, but I can sometimes go an entire day without eating a single vegetable. I love ice cream, but I don't ever feel like eating the whole pint in one sitting anymore. I love peanut butter on toast for breakfast, but I never binge on the entire jar like I used to. I don't have to worry about what to eat at dinner parties, and I don't have to research the menus of restaurants ahead of time. I don't weigh and measure my food. I enjoy a slice of cake at birthday parties. I eat my burgers with buns. I rarely overeat. And on an occasion when I do, I'm totally OK with it because I know it's not a reflection of my own failure.

Once I was no longer trying to control my food intake, I no longer lost control, either.

As for my health, the yo-yoing weight has stopped, the binge eating has stopped, and I've settled at a stable weight for my body. Sure, it isn't the thin body I'd spent my life trying to achieve, but I know I am healthier and happier than when I was stuck in the prison of dieting and food fear.

Throughout this journey, I've had to redefine what healthy means to me, and what I think it looks like. The next step in this journey details how important it was for me to change my perspective about my health and the health of those around me.

Step 3:

Redefine Healthy

I think we can all agree that our health is important and being healthy is great. But when it comes to what a healthy body should look like, the widespread cultural ideal is limited to a very narrow range.

The belief that a "healthy body" is only someone who is lean and muscular is not something we're born with. We've been fed this idea of society's perfect body our whole lives from television, magazines, the Internet and even medical professionals. The further we are from the body ideal, the further we must be from health, right?

Wrong. Healthy bodies come in all sizes, and they certainly aren't limited to the largely unattainable athletic body type that's featured on magazine covers and nutritional advertisements. And the assumption that leaner equals healthier simply is not true. You know who's feeding us this falsehood over and over? The same industries that are profiting from our insecurities and keeping us wanting something we can't attain so we'll continue buying the "magic pills" we hope will get us there.

If you fundamentally feel like you need to lose weight first in order to be healthy, then it's time to start redefining what healthy means to you.

First step: Don't confuse weight loss with health. Health doesn't care about your size. Health is about freedom and self-care. Dieting, on the other hand, is about control. It's about controlling your size and making you smaller.

Self-care is drinking a green smoothie with your breakfast. Control is Shakeology or meal-replacement shakes.

Self-care is moving your body in a way that feels good and gives you energy and strength. Control is targeting your "trouble areas" or doing sit-ups to flatten your stomach.

Self-care is doing positive things to make you feel like the best version of yourself. Control is fighting yourself by denying your appetite or cravings, eating foods that don't satisfy you, or deciding that tomorrow you'll be that brand new, perfect person.

When I was eating my bunless burger, I was focused on control, not self-care. I wasn't sending my daughter a message about health. I was sending her a message about my size, and how important it was for me to be thin. I could eat all the salads and quinoa I wanted during the day, but after my kids went to bed and I raided the snack cabinet, my body wasn't rebelling against my desire to be healthy. It was rebelling against my desire to control.

When it comes to health, ditch control. Choose self-care.

• • •

"But I need to lose this weight if I'm ever going to be healthy."

Do you know what's much healthier than weight loss? Releasing your shame and guilt around food and your body.

Fact: Dieting and forced weight loss typically cause more health problems than they solve, simply because they are unsuccessful in the long term, mess with your metabolism and hormones, and often lead to more weight gain in the end. And all this happens despite your strong determination and willpower, which then leads to feelings of failure and despair, stress and depression. That's not healthy. In fact, frequent yo-yo dieters have a higher risk of cardiovascular disease and Type 2 diabetes than those of a stable-weight, even if they're heavier.[21]

As I mentioned in the first chapter, research now shows a longer life span in people who are classified as overweight or even in the first class of obesity. In fact, significant weight-related health problems only start to occur at the extreme ends of the weight spectrum (which are very small sections of the population). Even then, those health risks associated with obesity are just as likely to be related to behaviors, stress, and socio-economic status than with weight alone. No studies have been able to prove a causal relationship with weight and health, only a correlative one.

When a client says to me that she wants to lose weight, I typically ask her what that would entail. She'll say, "Oh, I would eat healthier and be more active." And hey, that's a great idea! But keep the focus on behaviors — not the scale.

"But the scale keeps me accountable and tells me I'm on the right track."

This might work in the short term, but eventually an obsession with that number can lead to restrictive eating behaviors, followed by frustration and low self-esteem when the number goes up despite your "hard work."

"Let me just lose the weight first, and then I'll focus on exercise and healthy habits in order to maintain the weight loss."

I've heard this so many times. Hell, I've thought this so many times. The problem is, actively losing weight when you're most likely to gain it all back and then some (leading to yet another diet) is actually doing damage to your health.

"I just feel better when I'm at a lower weight."

That might be the case, but again, actively seeking weight loss increases the likelihood that you'll weigh more in the end. There is absolutely no data to suggest that weight loss alone actually makes people healthier or improves longevity. So "feeling better" has a lot more to do with our social and cultural influences than our health (more on that in Chapter 5).

I encountered more than a few Weight Watchers members near tears as they talked about the damn scale. "I have more energy, my cholesterol is lower, my blood pressure is lower, but that number won't budge!"

If your obsession with weight loss is getting in the way of your happiness, then it's not healthy.

By switching your focus to improving your lifestyle habits, rather than weight loss, you're focusing on what truly matters — your health and wellness. By rejecting that number on the scale, you're confirming that it is irrelevant to who you are and how you feel.

And once you remove weight from the equation, ask yourself, "Am I practicing self-care or control? Am I doing this because I want to get healthy, or because I want to lose weight?" Always differentiate the two.

"But I can't possibly be healthy at my current size."

Have you ever gone to the doctor, and she tells you your blood pressure is great, your cholesterol is great, you're a picture of health, but … you need to lose weight? Or well-meaning family and friends might say, "I'm just worried about your health!" Your BMI chart says your overweight or obese, which must mean you can't possibly be healthy, right?

Enter Health at Every Size®. The HAES® movement was created by a group of health care professionals, scientists and other experts who have grown tired of the dogma that you must be thin to be healthy. They've collected mountains of research that proves an emphasis on weight loss and the BMI scale as a measure of one's health is severely limited and often harmful. The HAES® philosophy doesn't claim ALL sizes are healthy; it's based on a belief that health is achievable regardless of size. It's certainly not against weight loss, but it's against the intentional pursuit of weight loss.

HAES® healthcare professionals adhere to these five principals:

1. **Weight Inclusivity:** Accept and respect the inherent diversity of body shapes and sizes and reject the idealizing or pathologizing of specific weights.

2. **Health Enhancement:** Support health policies that improve and equalize access to information and services, and personal practices that improve

human well-being, including attention to individual physical, economic, social, spiritual, emotional, and other needs.

3. **Respectful Care:** Acknowledge our biases, and work to end weight discrimination, weight stigma, and weight bias. Provide information and services from an understanding that socio-economic status, race, gender, sexual orientation, age, and other identities impact weight stigma, and support environments that address these inequities.

4. **Eating for Well-being:** Promote flexible, individualized eating based on hunger, satiety, nutritional needs, and pleasure, rather than any externally regulated eating plan focused on weight control.

5. **Life-Enhancing Movement:** Support physical activities that allow people of all sizes, abilities, and interests to engage in enjoyable movement, to the degree that they choose.[22]

The BMI scale is BS

Did you know that the Body Mass Index scale used by doctors today was actually invented by a Belgian mathematician in the 1850s? Lambert Adolphe Jacques Quetelet wasn't interested in health or fitness when he invented the scale, which measures a person's weight relative to height. Instead, he wanted a quick and easy way to place large populations into size categories in order to find averages. It was never intended to be used on individuals, much less become the gold standard by which we measure our health today.

Fast forward to 1972, when Dr. Ancel Keys recommended it as a general measurement for an individual's body fat percentage in an article in The Journal of Chronic Diseases. Then the National Institutes of Health adopted it in 1985, and it's popularity grew.

Despite the fact that it had a 50 percent failure rate in determining a person's health based on where they rate on the BMI scale, and the fact that it doesn't measure important factors like fitness level or blood pressure, it has now become the most popular predictor in our society of whether we are a "normal" weight or not. Quick and easy for the win.

I remember hearing Linda Bacon talk about the history of the BMI scale on a podcast interview. She asked the interviewer to imagine a whole population of people who went to bed one night as perfectly healthy individuals and woke up to discover they were classified as overweight. That word carries a lot of stigma in our culture, and it's long been synonymous with "unhealthy."

But seriously, overweight from *what?*

Imagine if our society had an expanded view of what healthy looks like. Imagine if a pediatrician doesn't try to put a 3-year-old on a diet because her BMI is on the high side. What if it was simply assumed that the 3-year-old was a healthy, chubby, happy child, rather than fearing the child will only get fatter if we don't nip it in the bud early? Imagine if we looked at most bodies through this same lens — recognizing that there is no "normal" size and that we can assume nothing about a person's health simply by looking at their body size.

Perhaps that 3-year-old wouldn't develop a fear of food, or later turn to food to soothe her feelings of deprivation in life, or feel like she's somehow inherently bad or deficient because of her larger body size, feeling socially ostracized, which then turns to eating for comfort, which leads to shame, which then leads to dieting and weight-cycling and failure and more shame and overeating and weight gain and blame and discrimination and more failure and overeating and depression and guilt and repeat, repeat, repeat!

It's not our bodies that need to change. It's our views, and society's view, of what is acceptable. Would you tell someone with very dark skin to simply lighten their skin if they want to eradicate racism? No, you battle systemic racism. But we regularly tell overweight people to shrink rather than trying to fix the widespread misbelief that they're not healthy, and therefore somehow not worthy of basic human respect and dignity.

• • •

It's true, not every size is healthy. It's pretty safe to

assume that a 75-pound woman with an eating disorder or a 500-pound bedridden man are not at their optimal health. But for the most part, health exists in a MUCH wider range than our culture is willing to represent. And the harder we all try to stuff ourselves and our kids into the "normal" BMI range, the more likely we are to screw up our bodies and slide farther and farther away from our goal.

When a weight-specific lens is applied to health, all of the other contributing factors affecting an individual's well-being tend to get lost in the process. My Weight Watchers members were glad when they felt great, but they simply couldn't shake the belief that they weren't at their optimal health until they reached their coveted goal weight. And my job as their leader was to encourage this belief, to make sure they keep striving for weight loss for *their health*. (Oh, and also because the company won't make any money off you if you're simply healthy. You have to get to that magic imaginary number first. Good luck with that!)

When it comes to the Health At Every Size® approach, I've heard many health care professionals say: "Once you've been HAESed, you can't be un-HAESed." The philosophy makes so much sense, it becomes impossible to return to your old beliefs.

What I love about the approach is that it shifts the focus away from the assumption that size has anything to do with health, and instead supports the idea that achieving "health" comes down to each person's

unique habits, behaviors, mental well-being, satisfaction, relationships, socio-economic status, career,
treatment by their peers, spiritual well-being and so
much more.

And nobody in the movement is pro-obesity, because there are some health problems that weight
loss undoubtedly alleviates, such as joint pain and
osteoarthritis. But HAES® recognizes that the majority of health problems that are currently blamed
on obesity, such as diabetes and high blood pressure,
can be effectively treated with a focus on lifestyle
changes not linked to weight loss. Moreover, a focus
on weight loss may actually be counterproductive
and hazardous to our health when we're continually
battling our weight.

So rather than thinking "I can't possibly be healthy,"
ask yourself, "What does the word 'healthy' mean
for me?"

Change the channel

Images and media are especially influential when it
comes to internalizing our ideas of what is normal.
But in a size-obsessed culture of "beach ready" bodies and weight loss "success stories," our brains are
bombarded with the singular message over and over
again: We're not good enough they way we are, but
we can fix ourselves if we buy what they're selling!

When I was constantly dieting, my social media

feeds consisted of two themes: body goals and food. I was convinced I could remain inspired to reach my weight goal by scrolling through a constant stream of #fitspo messages about working hard, getting to the gym, achieving those washboard abs, and earning myself a body worthy of showing off.

Since I was always in a state of restriction, I was also obsessed with food. I would ogle over any and all accounts that featured beautiful photos of "spiralized" zucchini noodles, Whole 30-approved meals, açai smoothie bowls or sugar-free black bean brownies or whatever else I thought I needed to eat in order to achieve optimal health.

When these images are all you see, it's hard not to believe in this extremely narrow view of healthy food and healthy bodies, as well as the moral imperative to always be working harder.

One of the best things I did for my mental well-being was to curate my Instagram feed, getting rid of the food and the hard bodies and adding body-positive accounts that celebrated all shapes and sizes.

I saw images of plus-sized women participating fully in life and (gasp) being happy with themselves! This is so rarely shown in our current culture. Think about it. Fat people are almost always shown in the media as unhappy, looking longingly at junk food, either trying hard to lose weight or acting morally repugnant if they're not. Or we see them simply as "headless fatties" in articles used to warn us of what's inevitable if we don't stay fit, eat right and help wage the "war on obesity."

If we see a thin woman in a movie eating ice cream to soothe a broken heart, we empathize with her pain. If we see a fat woman eating ice cream, we think, "No wonder you're fat. No wonder you're single."

In order to change my own discriminatory beliefs, I chose to follow women who don't give a crap about the negative portrayal of fat people. They refuse to feel bad about themselves, and they celebrate their bodies. They're giving a giant middle finger to the same culture that has told them their whole lives that they are ugly and unworthy of love and respect. As I expanded my definition of the beautiful body, the way I looked at myself and others was radically altered.

Whenever I find myself in a grocery store, at Target, or anywhere with a lot of people, I challenge myself to stop focusing on the thin women around me, wishing I could look like them. Instead, I make a point of looking around at the other women. The women with bodies of all sizes. The women who look like me. These women lead full lives. They have goals and families and they need to be seen. They make up the majority of us, and it doesn't serve us to ignore their existence or their worth.

It's time to change the channel. Clear your social media feed of messages that dictate how a woman should look. Put down the fitness magazines. Stop trying to mold your body into something it's not. Cook real pasta. Embrace yourself for who you are. End the war with your body, and you'll have no reason to rebel.

In the next chapter, I talk about how learning to accept my body as it is right now lead me toward better health and a body I could finally being to love and respect.

Step 4:

Live in the Body

You Have

"and i said to my body. softly. 'i want to be your friend.' it took a long breath. and replied 'i have been waiting my whole life for this." — *Nayyirah Waheed*

My closet was always stuffed with clothes that didn't fit me. Some were too small but I held onto them because I knew one day I'd be able to wear them again. Or they were too large, but I feared I'd eventually be back to that size.

I also had a habit of buying clothing I liked, even if they were too small, because I figured they'd offer me an incentive to lose a few pounds. "Goal clothes."

One thing was constant: The body I had in the present moment was never my "actual" body. It wasn't the true me.

Even at my thinnest, I still wanted to lose weight. *I was always unhappy with my body*. I was insecure. I wanted to get rid of my cellulite and tone my stomach. There were always more flaws to find. I used to think, "Once I do this or that, then I'll be happy with my body." But that never happened. I actually became more unhappy than ever before.

In fact, whenever I thought about trying to love my body, I worried that by doing so I would lose all motivation to "get fixed."

How right I was.

When we are dissatisfied with our bodies, we forever remain dissatisfied. The only thing that brings happiness with your body is being satisfied with it just as it is now. This doesn't mean you can't improve it or nourish it or challenge it. But it does mean that you accept it for what it is today, and treat it with the respect it deserves right now.

The belief that we are flawed and need to be fixed is so ingrained, we don't even question it. If we don't focus on our flaws, we'll never improve, right?

But what if you just decide to be flawless?

Sure, it's easier said than done. I spent a lifetime being unhappy with my body, so it was impossible for me to wake up one day and suddenly love it (or even like it). But my journey started with the simple act of not hating it.

How to not hate your body

First, start by viewing your body as a hard-working machine. Focus on all the ways in which your body is working to help and heal you.

Think about your body temperature, which your body needs to keep within a certain range for optimal health. When you get a fever, it's your body's way of telling you that it's fighting an infection. When you're hot, you sweat as a way to cool down your internal thermostat. When you're cold, you shiver to heat yourself up.

Think about your cuts, and how your body creates extra cells and scar tissue to heal you. Or how your mouth gets dry when you're in need of hydration. Think about your grumbling stomach, and how your body lets you know it needs fuel and nutrition to keep the gears running smoothly. Full bladder, head ache, arousal, adrenaline — these are all functions of the body that are meant to heal us, warn us, please us, and keep us safe.

Your body does all this without being told. You're not in control of these functions. It's foolish to think you are. Imagine if someone told you you're not breathing properly and you need to change it. You might be able to do it for a while, but eventually you'd gasp for air and have to give in to your body's natural function. Or imagine if you decided you would only use the bathroom at a certain time every day. Or you thought you blinked too much, so you tried to only blink once per minute. These sound ridiculous, but that's exactly the sort of control we try to wield over our body when we diet and restrict and refuse to listen to our natural hunger and fullness cues.

Your body spends 100 percent of its time healing you, and keeping you alive and healthy. *That's all it does.* Take a moment to thank it, and give it some respect and recognition for keeping you alive this long, despite all the crap and criticism you've heaped on it.

It's not our job to tell our bodies how to feel, breathe, or heal. It's also not our job to tell our bodies what size they should be. Get out of your own way and let your body do its thing.

Act like an anthropologist

Try viewing your habits from a place of objective investigation. Pretend you're an anthropologist studying human behavior, only this time it's your own. This is a great way to remove the judgment and stigma inherent in our behaviors.

Perhaps you just ate half a dozen donuts. You beat yourself up: "Ugh, I'm a disgusting glutton with no self-control who will never figure out this eating thing no matter how hard I try. I'm so uncomfortable and I hate myself and why can't I just be a normal eater like everyone else? What is wrong with me?!"

Sound familiar? How does that serve you? Does it make you work harder next time? Does it really change your behaviors in the future? How many times have you vowed to be better yet ended up right back in the same situation?

Try approaching this same act from an anthropologist's point of view: "I ate six donuts today. I told myself I'd just have one, but I couldn't stop. I was craving one when I started, and my guilt and judgment led me to eat the rest. I now feel stuffed and uncomfortable. I will likely not be hungry for dinner, or maybe I will be. Either way, I've learned something about myself and my body, and it's highly unlikely that I'll eat another six donuts tomorrow (but if I do, I'll simply re-evaluate then)."

See the difference when judgment is left out of the equation and you can simply evaluate the actions? We can be curious about our feelings and our experiences, and when you step back from the situation and release yourself from any guilt, shame or negative judgment, it becomes a lot easier to neutralize the behavior and figure out where it's coming from.

The same goes for how you view your body. In fact, body dissatisfaction actually has a stronger negative health effect than actually being fat. Women with body dissatisfaction tend to have worse health than women who don't feel bad about their weight, regardless of their size.[23]

Whenever you're angry with your body, try taking

a moment to simply evaluate your thoughts with non-judgmental awareness and try to turn that thought into a neutral statement. For example, "My stupid fat thighs are always rubbing together" could be turned into "My thighs are strong and help me walk. How can I help them feel comfortable?" Or "My doctor told me I'm pre-diabetic and now I'm screwed. Why have I been such an idiot?" could be turned into "My body is sending me a message and now my role is to help it heal."

Move away from the "What is wrong with me?!" approach, and instead try the "This is who I am" approach. When you feel neutral about your body, you can build an appreciation for what it can do for you now, rather than wishing it looked or acted differently.

Remind yourself of the strengths of your body and how it got you to where you are today. Treat your body with respect, and appreciate it for the amazing machine it is. This will help you begin to move from a state of dissatisfaction with your body to a place of acceptance.

Also, remind yourself that what's above your neck and what's below your neck are interconnected, and the food you choose to eat affects your body. It makes up your cells and helps regenerate your organs. You literally are what you eat. From this place, you can begin to feed your body the best food you can, be patient and begin to trust yourself again.

As we take better care of ourselves through nourishing practices and develop more appreciation and kindness toward our bodies, we leave room to hear what they are telling us. Once we are listening and receptive, we can respond accordingly.

Body appreciation doesn't come from losing weight. Appreciation comes from being in a positive relationship with your body and knowing how to take care of it. Ask yourself this: How do you treat something you appreciate versus something you hate?

Your body was never a problem to be fixed

For the last two years, I've coached for Girls on the Run. The program was developed for young girls and teens to give them skills to help them navigate social situations, their emotions, bullying and gossip, while also developing an appreciation for health and fitness.

Each 10-week program culminates with girls positively impacting their communities through a service project and being physically and emotionally prepared to complete a 5K.

Many girls who sign up have never run before in their lives, yet they finish the 5K. They run, they walk, they skip. The thrill and pride in their eyes when they cross the finish line is incredible to witness.

The following is a letter I wrote to my girls, who are aged 8 through 11. I'm including it here because I believe it applies to all of us at any age:

To my Girls on the Run girls,

We are so often told that we are either too much of something or not enough. Lots of companies make millions of dollars telling us that there is something wrong with us. They want to convince us that we are broken, so we will buy whatever they're offering that will fix us. We get these messages everywhere — in magazines, on television, on social media, on the Internet.

After a while, we start to internalize these messages. We start to believe something is wrong with us and that we need to be fixed. This chips away at our self-confidence and makes us feel bad about ourselves. And when we look around at others, we believe there is something wrong with them. Sometimes we even tell them something is wrong with them, because we think it might make us feel better about ourselves. But it doesn't work. Do you know why?

Because you are not broken. You don't need to be fixed.

You are not too tall.
You are not too short.

You are not too fat.
You are not too thin.

You are not too loud.
You are not too quiet.

You are not too silly.
You are not too serious.

You are not too smart.
You are not too dumb.

You are not too shy.
You are not too confident.

You are not too lazy.
You are not too busy.

You are not too girly.
You are not not girly enough.

You are not too fast.
You are not too slow.

You are perfect just as you are.

So repeat after me:

"There is nothing wrong with me. I am exactly who I am supposed to be. And I am capable of great things. I am worthy of respect simply because I'm me."

And when you look at the girls around you, remember they are exactly who they are supposed to be. They are capable of great things, they are perfect, and they are worthy of respect.

With love and gratitude,
Coach Katy

It feels so easy to give this important message to young girls, but so difficult to believe it for ourselves. What if you treated yourself like you would a young girl? What would you say to that girl about her body? What would you say to her about her worth in this world? What you say to her if she told you she felt about her body the way you feel about your own?

Let yourself go

The phrase "Oh dear, she's really let herself go" conjures up for me a small gaggle of women whispering about someone who has gained weight. I'm sure we've all heard this phrase muttered at some point in our lives, or we've even thought it about someone else.

Nobody wants to be the woman everyone else is pitying. That's why we try so hard to control our bodies. It's never been about our health; it has always been about our place in society and our ability to be accepted or even praised by others.

The phrase "letting yourself go" has such a negative connotation, as though we all fear that if we stop trying to control our bodies and let go, somehow chaos and misery will ensue. But in reality, the opposite is true. Once you begin to trust your body and understand it and accept it for what it is, you can be free of the torment and chaos, and happiness can be restored.

It's time to break the chains, and embrace yourself for who you are. Let others marvel at you with envy as they exclaim, "Wow! She's really let herself go!"

Fat phobia and the price of fat shaming

The average weight of Americans has climbed considerably over the past 30 years. A recent study found 71 percent of American men and 62 percent of women are now classified as overweight (having a BMI greater than 25).[24] While more men are overweight, women are more likely to be classified as obese (having a BMI greater than 30), with the rate at 40.4 percent compared to 35 percent of men.

When it comes to kids, nearly 30 percent of boys and girls under age 20 are considered overweight, up from 19 percent in the late 1980s. The childhood obesity rates have tripled — with the rates of obese 6- to 11-year-olds more than doubling (from 7 percent to 17.5 percent) and rates of obese teens quadrupling from 5 percent to 20.5 percent.

In a nation where we all know how to eat well and be active, why are we gaining weight? After all, we are bombarded with warnings about the dangers weight poses to our health, and society has made it clear to fat people that they are shameful, unlovable, and in desperate need of intervention. So why would anyone in this culture continue to be fat when we all find it so appalling?

There are dozens of theories, from the prevalence of fast food and processed food to our general inactivity or sheer laziness. We can blame genetic predisposition, socio-economic status, lack of education or limited access to fresh food. But there's one thing everyone seems to agree on: Nobody wants to be fat. And if you are fat, you will be chastised and insulted every day for the rest of your life until you finally shape up and lose weight.

And when fat people stand up and defend themselves, asking that they be treated like regular human beings with basic rights and dignities, we call it "glorifying obesity."

When fat people ask for more full-figured models and more representation in the media, or more clothing options in regular department stores, the general reaction is: Well, if we "normalize" fatness, if we allow them to feel happy and accepted in society, then we are condoning fatness and they will keep getting fatter and fatter.

We believe that the best way to treat obesity in our society is to demonize the fat person, bully them into submission, mock them, blame them, shun them, ignore their needs.

We believe that fat people don't deserve happiness, because happiness will make them fatter. Instead, we make sure they know that happiness is not something they deserve, and that their worth is not inherent.

They're told every day in thousands of ways that they should lose weight if they want to be happy, and they're lazy failures if they can't figure out how to do it. And not surprisingly, they internalize this belief and wonder, "Why am I such a lazy failure?"

If we spend so much time demonizing weight and obesity, then why are we only getting fatter? I mean, education, public shaming and ostracizing worked with smokers, so why doesn't it work with fat people?

For one thing, you can live without smoking. You can't live without food. For another thing, food becomes the one thing to comfort us from the constant shame and humiliation we face for being fat. And finally, our bodies are built to gain weight, not lose weight. It's a matter of survival. The more we mess with this biological system, the more likely we are to increase our set point weights over time.

In my experience, the heaviest Weight Watchers members were almost always the hardest working dieters, yet they inherently believed they were lazy and lacked willpower. They came back over and over trying to figure out how to get better, how to be normal, how to finally like themselves again.

We must stop bullying heavier people, especially kids. Weight is the most common reason children are bullied in school.[25] In one study, nearly 85 percent of adolescents reported seeing overweight classmates teased in gym class.[26]

Fat shaming isn't working. It's inhuman and misguided. We must stop acting like being fat is the worst thing in the world. It isn't.

If a kid calls herself fat, as her parent you might want to say, 'Don't be silly! You're beautiful!' But what you're actually saying is, "Being fat is horrible, and I don't think you're horrible."

The more we stigmatize fatness, the more our children will fear it and the harder they will try to stay thin as a means toward loving themselves and finding acceptance. This means harmful dieting, eating disorders, poor self image and, almost always, a never-ending cycle of emotional eating, weight gain, self-loathing, and dieting. Repeat ad nauseam.

Ending fatphobia is not the same as "glorifying obesity." Instead, it's about treating fat people with dignity and making sure that all sizes of people are worthy of love and acceptance.

Put simply: The less we fear being fat, the less likely we are to become fat.

And even if we do become fat, does that make us any less worthy of love, respect and basic human dignity?

Imagine a world where girls were told that it was OK to love their bodies at every size. They would never have to diet at age 10 to battle their perfectly natural adolescent pudge, never have a pediatrician announce that at age 5 their BMI was too high and their parents should probably cut back on the sweets.

They might actually grow up to be healthy, happy and self-confident, instead of being convinced their worth and their ability to be loved depended entirely on the size of their bodies. They might actually have a simple, healthy relationship with food, instead of fearing it, craving it, restricting it and overcompensating with binges.

They might actually believe they are perfect just as they are and accept their body's natural size, rather than desperately trying to shrink it. What a beautiful world that would be.

Step 5:

Exercise Compassion

"Workout because you love your body, not because you hate it." If you google this quote, it comes up as a mantra on tons of fitness sites. But what does it actually mean, especially for those of us who no longer want to participate in diet culture?

Rediscover your sense of play

Physical fitness is a major contributor to health. When I talk about changing lifestyle habits, moving your body is an important one, especially given the benefits to your cardiovascular and musculoskeletal health, not to mention the endorphins that improve your mood and sense of self worth.

But simply knowing the benefits of exercise doesn't always get us up and moving. Many of us have come to look at exercise as a chore, something we really *should* be doing more of, something that's supposed to be difficult (no pain, no gain!). Even the term "workout" implies that somehow this is serious business and not at all relaxing.

Have you ever watched children at a playground? My own kids will complain incessantly that they're tired whenever we walk anywhere, but the minute we get to a playground, they find the energy to scale the monkey bars and play tag for hours. Are they doing this because they're trying to work on their abs or get rid of cellulite? Of course not. They're having fun, and their little bodies are experiencing joyful movement.

Another reason we avoid exercise is because we tend to view it as a means to weight loss, which it isn't. When we start a new diet and vow to change our life through health and wellness, we get really pumped about joining a gym or starting a new exercise routine. But the excitement rarely lasts long. We're exhausted and the work isn't producing the "results" we were hoping for. So we start to find excuses: I'm too tired. I don't have time. The gym is too far.

Rather than thinking of exercise as a "workout," change the way you view it. "Joyful movement" flips the script when it comes to physical fitness. When I think of joyful movement, I think of my kids at the playground. I think of swimming with them in the pool, or going for bike rides on the rail trail. I think of hiking through the woods, or playing frisbee, or dance parties in the kitchen.

These are all things we love to do as a family, and the incorporation of movement feels secondary to the fact that we're together enjoying the outdoors or bopping to music. We're never thinking about weight loss, which makes it feel like quality time rather than a chore.

Concentrate on what your body can do, not on how it looks

Movement gives you more energy, helps your blood circulate, strengthens your muscles and bones. But it stops being fun when it's done with the intent to change what your body looks like.

Exercise is another example of self-care versus control. Joyful movement is an act of self-care. Targeting your "trouble zones" is an act of control. If you find yourself criticizing your body, pushing it too hard, lecturing yourself that you *should* do a certain amount of exercise each week because it's good for you, then you've lost the sense of joy and replaced it with a sense of perfectionism. Plus, you risk being overtired and stressing your body, which could lead to injury (and your body will likely try to protect itself through, you guessed it, weight gain).

This doesn't necessarily mean you should avoid the gym or workout classes. I love Zumba, mostly because I magically transform into a Latin diva (as long as there are no mirrors around). As the music pumps and I try to keep up with the confusing fast-paced moves, I'm never thinking about my muscle definition or even how ridiculous I look (I'm not a sweaty, red-faced, hot mess. I'm a Latin diva, damn it!). I'm simply in the moment and appreciating my jerky legs and flailing arms for getting me through the routine.

Find something you love to do, and challenge yourself and your body in ways that make you feel good to be alive, rather than counting the minutes until it's over and you're back home in bed. If your gym instructor is telling you to target your belly fat or work off that cupcake, or you're being pushed so hard you want to puke, it might be time to ditch the membership and focus on other ways to optimize your well-being.

Simply getting up and moving each day is all we really need to stay healthy. Anything beyond that can quickly turn into negatively pushing yourself, controlling your body and fixating on its flaws or limitations.

If walking is not available to you, never underestimate the health benefits — both mental and physical — of a good solo dance party. Put on your favorite music and shake your booty. Bonus: You can do it in your underwear! Even if it feels totally goofy or you think you're a lousy dancer, the mere act of dancing allows you to become connected to your body as you follow the rhythm of your favorite song. As my daughter once noted, "It's hard to be in a bad mood when your favorite music is playing."

Yoga and meditation for diet recovery

I first discovered yoga back in the late 1990s. I was instantly drawn to it, mostly because I was naturally flexible and it was something I was good at it, despite my larger body. I didn't know much about the mental and emotional benefits at the time. I just liked how I felt afterwards, and I was proud of what my body could do.

Over the years, I would drift away and then return to yoga practice. I always felt good when I was practicing regularly, but I also allowed my diet-culture mindset to infiltrate my practice.

I began to look at my yoga instructors not as my guides through the practice, but as the body type to which I aspired. "If I keep this up and come regularly, I'll look just like my hot teacher!" I would glance around at the other students in the class, wondering if they were watching me as I awkwardly tried to shove my legs into something resembling pigeon pose. I would curse my stiffness if I could no longer achieve a pose that I could easily do in the past. If the teacher suggested a way to "take this pose further," I always pushed myself to the limits to prove to myself that I could do it.

The same competitive and perfectionist voice — the one that had been telling me for years that my body wasn't good enough, that I needed to lose weight, that I needed to work harder — led me to dread going to a class because I feared I wasn't thin enough or that I lacked flexibility. I felt anxious about whether I looked OK in my poses. I would get frustrated if I needed assistance with yoga blocks. I was embarrassed if I got sweaty.

I'd worry if I had the right clothes or the best yoga mat or how long I could "ommmm." Rather than concentrating on the short- and long-term physical benefits of the practice or feeling good in my body in the present moment, yoga had become just another form of exercise that I was "not in the mood for."

But yoga is so much more than exercise, despite how aggressive and competitive the culture has become in some circles. Yoga allows us to re-connect with our bodies in a world where disconnection with and disapproval of our bodies is cultivated continuously by diet culture.

If you've ever been in a yoga class, you'll hear the instructor talk about slowing down your mind and connecting your body and breath. Yoga helps you turn inward, paying attention to your body with curiosity rather than judgment. When your teacher tells you to root your feet to the floor and lift your toes, you can't help but concentrate on your toes instead of your grocery list. You're giving attention to a body part in a new way, using focus and discipline. Otherwise, we too easily glide through our days, listening to our thoughts and ignoring what's going on below the neck.

Being "in your body" this way, you can slowly start to transform your thoughts about what your body can do for you, which begins to cultivate respect for your body. Rather than pushing yourself to perfect a pose or competing with others in the class, allow yourself to simply listen to your body in each pose, adopting a kind and generous attitude toward yourself in the process.

Mild discomfort is also part of yoga (not to be confused with actual pain), and it can have an amazing effect on your mind/body relationship when in diet recovery. When holding a pose for what seems like forever, ask yourself "Is this pose uncomfortable, and how long can I sit with this discomfort?" Sitting with discomfort is another way to return to the breath and listen to your body while being in the moment. Often when we pay any attention to our body, it's through our thoughts and opinions of it, rather than simply listening to it.

For every person who says, "I'm not flexible enough for yoga," this is exactly why you need to try it. Yoga is about meeting yourself wherever you are without any intent to change. It's about you and your body together on the mat in the present moment.

Another way of practicing being in the moment is through meditation. Even if it's just for 5 or 10 minutes a day, meditation has been proven to help with a number of mental and physical health conditions, including anxiety and depression.[27]

If you've avoided meditation because you thought you didn't have time or that you're not good at it (or it's just too weird), start slowly by taking a few minutes each day. Collect your thoughts and clear your mind either through attention to your breathing or repeating a phrase or mantra. Clearing your mind of thoughts and being entirely in the present moment, even for a few minutes a day, gives us a respite from our fears, anxieties, perfectionism and self-criticism.

And remember, there's no wrong way to meditate. No matter how many times your mind wanders, bringing yourself back to the present moment is the essence of meditation. Each time we return to the breath or the mantra, it's like building a muscle that allows you to tune out the voices in your head and separate yourself from them. By tuning out the negative body image voices and returning to the present moment, you can feel neutral about your body, if only for a few minutes a day.

The importance of rest

Newsflash: You don't have to be healthy. You don't have to be anything.

This mentality of "I should eat healthy" and "I should exercise" comes from the same inner desire to be accepted in society — to be good and *be obedient* — that led to our diet voice in the first place. Hearing these "should" thoughts in our heads over and over for years and years can be exhausting, and it's important to make time for plenty of rest when you are recovering from dieting.

When I stopped dieting, I also gave up rigorous exercise. I needed to stop pushing myself and to redefine what it meant to really take care of myself.

After years of diets, my body had slowed my metabolism to conserve energy. My workouts were mostly fueled by adrenaline, not food. Once I started eating again, my metabolism needed time to repair itself.

In addition to being hungry, I was exhausted. So I slept. A lot.

Whenever I took a nap, the voices in my head told me I was being lazy. I felt guilty for not accomplishing more. I was beating myself up over taking time to heal. I felt depressed. Not exactly the picture of health.

But the reason I called this chapter "Exercise Compassion" is because, as important as physical activity is to our health, it's equally important to listen to our bodies when it's time to take a break. Just as our bodies tell us when we need to stretch, or when we need to dance or yawn, our bodies are tired for a reason. Worry, anxiety, depression, and trying to desperately control ourselves can sap our energy. It's important that we take time to heal.

The more you make room for rest in your life, the

easier it becomes to find real energy and a willingness to move in ways you love. After a few months, I began to crave moving my body again, not because of the "shoulds" or worry that I was gaining weight, but because I genuinely felt like moving my body. I had returned to the state of the child in the playground, happiest when I was taking part in the life I had rather than trying to earn a better one.

However you find ways to move your body, find the joy and remember to have self-compassion. Our bodies are all so different, but they're each an amazing machine that is built to heal and to help us. Treat your body with love and respect and maintain a relationship of gratitude rather than expectation.

Now go put on some tunes and shake that rump.

Step 6:

Food & Body Freedom

Here we are at the final essential step: Food and body freedom. And when I say "freedom," I'm not talking about running through a field of daisies without a care in the world (although, if you manage to achieve that, let me know because it sounds amazing). Freedom means acceptance. You've searched other options, and this one feels right to you.

We are not our thoughts

Will I ever be rid of that voice inside me that tells me I'm fat, I'm a failure, I'm unlovable? After a lifetime of cultural conditioning, I don't think I will. But I have been able to turn down the volume by not giving it attention when it speaks up. Freedom is being able to go about my day unencumbered by that voice, regardless of what it's telling me.

A great way to shut down the voice is to ask yourself,

"What if this were my daughter or my friend saying this to herself? What would I tell her?" Chances are you'd be heartbroken to hear it from someone you love. Instead of immediately placing judgment on yourself, simply acknowledge the voices and ask yourself, "What would I say to a young girl or a friend?" Freedom means being your own best friend.

Food freedom

What is food freedom? It's actually pretty simple. Food freedom means eating with joy and never wondering if you should or shouldn't be eating something.

It means taking what you want, and stopping when you're full.

It means being attentive to your nutritional needs and your emotional needs, and trusting that there is no wrong way to feed yourself.

It means giving yourself permission to eat sometimes because you're bored, or sad, or just because you want to.

It means recognizing that there are no bad foods or good foods. You're not "being good" when you're sticking to a diet, and you're not a bad person if you aren't always eating the healthiest foods possible. There's no room for guilt with food freedom.

It means eating three meals or day, or six, or just snacking all day.

It means sometimes overeating, or skipping a meal, but trusting yourself to return to a normal state.

The more permission you give yourself to eat food, the less likely you are to eat out of control. Conversely, the more you avoid certain foods you love, and the more guilt and judgment you have around your food choices, the more likely you are to stress out and be miserable around food, which can adversely affect your health.

Food freedom doesn't require will power, and there is no regret. Lose the guilt and the judgment — they're just more ways of restricting yourself.

Food can be enjoyed, and your body can to be trusted. When it comes to true health, it's necessary to eat what you love and *as much as you want*.

Remember, you've been dieting for a long time, emotionally and physically, and that means your body has been in a state of semi-starvation. It is normal to eat more than you think you should, and this will pass. Trust the process and do not try to restrict. Your body will thank you.

Bodies don't make bad decisions. They let you know when you're hungry, when you're full, when you need to stretch, when you need to rest, and when you need to move. Listen to yours when it comes to making choices that support it.

When you stop fighting yourself and start listening, your body starts naturally and effortlessly achieving and maintaining a healthy weight.

Body freedom

If you could wave a magic wand and no longer have body image issues, how might your life be different? How much time and energy are you spending focusing on how your body looks? What else could you be doing?

If I meet another woman who refuses to wear a swimsuit because she's insecure, I will scream.

Look, I get it. I've done a lot of work on accepting my body, and yet every single time I look in the mirror, I think, "You're too fat. You need to lose weight."

Every. Single. Time.

But rather than going on yet another diet for the millionth time, I now take a minute to evaluate where that voice is coming from, and what I'm willing to do about it.

Am I willing to start counting calories again? No.
Am I willing to skip meals or reduce portions? No.
Am I willing to drink more water? Sure.
Am I willing to increase my activity levels? No, I'm

happy with my activity levels.

Am I willing to go to sleep earlier? Yes.

Am I willing to let my current size interfere with my happiness? No.

And so on.

This process brings me back to my health and away from my size, something I really don't have much control over. As long as I feel like I am looking out for my health, then I take the focus away from my dissatisfaction with my body.

Body freedom means every time you see a thin woman and think, "God, I wish I looked like her," you follow up with "But I don't, and that's OK, because I'm me and I'm pretty damn spectacular."

It means putting on the bathing suit no matter how uncomfortable it makes you, and participating in life because it would be tragic to do otherwise.

It means letting go of your "dream body" and telling yourself that life is too damn short to spend another minute agonizing over the size of your current body.

It means self-care, not control.

It means realizing that fighting your body has left you with nothing but misery, insecurity, and likely a binge eating problem, so now it's time to try something else and trust that you'll make it through.

It means being OK with the fact that there are going to be good days and bad days, but you're on the right path to healing as long as you're working with your body and not against it.

It means looking at your reflection and saying, "I'm sorry I've been so mean to you over the years."

It means not spending as much time fixated on how you look because you're too busy living your awesome life.

It means letting go of weight loss. I've tried. You've tried. And we've all failed over and over again. The only thing we can control is how we treat ourselves and our bodies. You don't have a weight-control problem, you have a self-love problem.

Conclusion

This is not where I say, "See? It's that easy! All you have to do is follow my *6 Essential Steps* and I guarantee you'll be happy and healthy forever!"

I wish it was that easy. But letting go of dieting and choosing to embrace my body is hands down the hardest thing I've ever tried. And I'm still in the muck of it all, always trying to break free of diet culture's hold on me.

Sometimes I honestly wish I'd never heard about Health at Every Size® or body positivity or the harmfulness of dieting. I wish I could just go back to my naive old self. She was so hopeful and determined. She worked hard and never gave up trying. It feels like I'm in mourning over losing her.

Sometimes I feel like an addict in recovery, longing for the high that dieting and weight loss brings. I lie awake at night, wanting to weigh myself "just this once." I miss the excitement of a new diet. It's such a rush to start that "new life," making changes, putting your best foot forward and finally getting your act together. Weight loss brings attention, confidence, smaller clothes — it's a powerful drug. But I now know that the high never lasts, and that the aftermath will leave me feeling broken and humiliated.

The only thing that's broken with us is that inner voice — the one that constantly tells us we're too fat, that we need to lose weight and that we'll never be happy until we do. And while we can't make the voice go away completely, we can make sure that we never give it the power it once had over us.

For years, I was in a diet prison and I was miserable. Eventually the time came when being happy and sane became more important to me than losing weight.

I started listening to another voice in my head, the quiet one in the background that said, "You know what? You're doing the best you can. You've gotten this far, and you're pretty awesome and strong."

Maybe this place of self-acceptance isn't as exciting or as thrilling as dieting, but there's a balance and a peace. The pendulum that once swung wildly between excitement and disappointment has finally stopped. I am enough just as I am.

• • •

I know I can't go back in time and tell my younger self that she's just fine the way she is, that her body is perfect and that she doesn't need to change or lose weight to be worthy of love and acceptance, and FOR CHRISSAKE, PUT DOWN THE SLIM FAST.

But I can tell my own daughter. And if I want her to believe it, then I need to believe it myself. This means giving myself full permission to be the person I am, to eat the foods I love and crave, and to treat my body with love and respect.

Self-care to me used to mean weight loss and striving to be better and fix my flaws. Now, self-care to me means being OK with myself and my body, and deciding that dammit, my flaws are who I am. Now I'm able to respect my body and take care of it. I'm not trying to hide it. I don't hate it anymore.

I even make a point of telling my daughter that I love my body. Whether or not I believe it, *she needs to hear it*. Lord knows I never heard it from any woman when I was growing up.

We were put on this planet to be so much more than just thin. We will not be worth more if we weigh less, and we were never broken objects that needed to be fixed.

• • •

In some ways, I'm grateful for my years as a "weight

loss success story." Before then, I was insecure about my body and I always felt like I was missing out on something — no matter how happy I was, I thought I'd be happier once I lost weight. I never believed I was enough.

Once I lost the weight, my life didn't magically become happier. In fact, I became even more insecure and unhappy, and much crazier around food.

After I broke free from dieting, I finally realized I had been perfectly fine all along. The only person who didn't see it was me.

I guess if you've made it this far in the book, then perhaps you're feeling like I am — that dieting isn't going to cut it anymore, but you feel scared to let go and just embrace yourself. I get it. I'm still going through it.

But at the end of the day, this is the only body you have. You can spend your life hating it and trying to change it, or you can try to repair your relationship and begin to appreciate it. It's not easy. It's really freaking hard. But knowing you're not alone and that you're not to blame can help you move forward.

You are so much more than your weight. You are perfect. You deserve to be happy.

Once you realize that the obsession with weight loss and the scale and "eating right" was causing your stress about food and your body, it will become easier to relax into a new style of intuitive eating, joyful movement, and peace with food.

And it does get easier. I promise. Saying goodbye to the merry-go-round of yo-yo dieting and binge eating, the blame and self-loathing, was like an enormous weight lifted off my shoulders.

This journey is worth it.

The woman on the left got a lot of compliments on how she looked. But she was also in a prison of her own making. She was obsessed with her weight, she chewed gum at parties to avoid eating, she weighed and measured portions, and she was still too self-conscious to wear a bikini . All she saw were her flaws — her stomach wasn't flat enough. She had too much cellulite. She'd feel much more confident if she could just fix her "trouble spots."

The woman on the right doesn't get as many compliments, but she's finally free. She eats whatever she wants, whenever she wants. She has embraced her body and appreciates all the wonderful things it does for her. She lives life to the fullest, and doesn't apologize for herself anymore. She's teaching her daughter to appreciate her own body and love it at every size and to never feel like she isn't enough. And oh yeah, she rocks a bikini, belly rolls and all.

Acknowledgments

This book could not have been written without my friends and family and my Worth It warriors, who supported and encouraged me along this amazing, tumultuous journey.

Many thanks to Domenica Murray, Julia May Jonas, Lauree Ostrofsky, Samantha Weber, and Peggy Belles for your feedback with earlier drafts.

Thank you to Joshna Maharaj and Caitlin Welles, whose lively and heartfelt conversations formed so many of the ideas behind this book.

And finally, my utmost gratitude to my husband, Matthew, who has listened to me rant and rave and cry, has debated with me and soothed me, and has loved and supported me unconditionally throughout. Thank you for always helping me find the right words. I love you.

About the Author

Katy is a recovering binge eater and chronic dieter who has struggled with disordered eating for 28 years and counting. As a certified health coach, Katy works with others who are ready to normalize their relationship with food and their body image and break free from the dieting and binge-eating cycle for good.

Katy supports her clients to make step-by-step changes to their food and lifestyle habits in a way that's enjoyable and easily integrated into their lives.

It's time to change your perspectives about your body, your health, and your self-worth. If you are ready to achieve food freedom and truly nourish your body from the inside out, visit *worthitwithkaty.com*.

Because you are worth it!

References

1 Bacon, Linda. "We're Wired to Maintain a Healthy Weight." Ezinearticles.com. Web. 10 April, 2009.

2 Tong, Jenny, and David D'Alessio. "Ghrelin and Hypothalamic Development: Too Little and Too Much of a Good Thing." The Journal of Clinical Investigation 125.2 (2015): 490–492. PMC. Web. 13 Sept. 2017.

3 Bacon, Linda. "We're Wired to Maintain a Healthy Weight." Ezinearticles.com. Web. 10 April, 2009.

4 Rosenbaum, Michael et al. "Energy Intake in Weight-Reduced Humans." Brain research 1350 (2010): 95–102. PMC. Web. 13 Sept. 2017.

5 Lowe, Michael R. et al. "Dieting and Restrained Eating as Prospective Predictors of Weight Gain." Frontiers in Psychology 4 (2013): 577. PMC. Web. 17 Aug. 2017.

6 Baker, David, and Keramidas, Natacha. "The psychology of eating." American Psychological Association, October 2013, vol 44, no. 9, page 66. Web.

7 Afzal S, Tybjærg-Hansen A, Jensen GB, Nordestgaard BG. Change in Body Mass Index Associated With Lowest Mortality in Denmark, 1976-2013. JAMA. 2016;315(18):1989–1996. doi:10.1001/jama.2016.4666

Flegal KM, Kit BK, Orpana H, Graubard BI. Association of All-Cause Mortality With Overweight and Obesity Using Standard Body Mass Index CategoriesA Systematic Review and Meta-analysis. JAMA. 2013;309(1):71–82. doi:10.1001/jama.2012.113905

8 Bacon, Linda and Aphramor, Lucy. "Weight Science: Evaluating the Evidence for a Paradigm Shift." Nutrition Journal, 2011, 10:9. Web.

9Mann, Tracy. "Oprah's Investment in Weight Watchers was Smart Because the Program Doesn't Work." nymag.com. New York Magazine. Web. 29 Oct. 2015.

10Doheny, Kathleen. "'Yo-Yo Dieting' Hard on Older Women's Hearts." WebMd. Web. 17 Nov., 2016.

11 David, Marc. "The Metabolic Power of Pleasure." Institute for the Psychology of Eating. Web. 2014.

12 Tylka, T.L., Calogero, R.M., & Danielsdottir S. (2015). "Is intuitive eating the same as flexible dietary control? Their links to each other and well-being could provide an answer." Appetite 95: 166-175.

13 Birch, Leann L., Johnson, Susan L., Andresen, Graciela, et al. "The Variability of Young Children's Energy Intake." The New England Journal of Medicine. Web. 24 Jan., 1991.

14 Satter, Ellen M. "Internal regulation and the evolution of normal growth as the basis for prevention of obesity in children." Journal of the American Dietetic Association. September 1996, vol 96, no. 9: 860-64.

15 Tribole, Evelyn, Resch, Elyse. "10 Principles of Intuitive Eating." intuitiveeating.org. Web. 2007-2017.

16 Roth, Geneen. "Kindness and Calories." geneenroth.com. Web. Sept. 2016.

17 Guyenet, Stephan. "Food Palatability and Body Fatness: Clues from Alliesthesia." Whole Health Source. Web. 18 August, 2011.

18 Schaefer, Julie T. et al. "A Review of Interventions that Promote Eating by Internal Cues." Journal of the Academy of Nutrition and Dietetics, vol. 114, Issue 5: 734-60. Web.

19 Bacon, Linda, Aphramor, Lucy. "Body Respect: What Conventional Health Books Get Wrong, Leave Out, and Just Plain Fail to Understand About Weight." BenBella Books, 2014. 66.

20 Bacon, Linda. "We're Wired to Maintain a Healthy Weight." Ezinearticles.com. Web. 10 April, 2009.

21 Bangalore, Sripal, Fayyad, Rana, et al. "Body-Weight Fluctuations and Outcomes in Coronary Disease." New England Journal of Medicine. Web. 6 April, 2017. 1332-40.

22 "The Health at Every Size Approach." sizediversityandhealth.org. Association for Size Diversity and Health. Web.

23 Bucchianeri, Michaela M. et al. "Body Dissatisfaction from Adolescence to Young Adulthood: Findings from a 10-Year Longitudinal Study." Body image 10.1 (2013): 10.1016/j. bodyim.2012.09.001. PMC. Web. 16 Aug. 2017.

24 Gregg, Edward W., Shaw, Jonathan E. "Global Health Effects of Overweight and Obesity." New England Journal of Medicine. 377:80-81. Web. DOI: 10.1056/NEJMe1706095.

25 Puhl, R.M., Latner, J.D., et al. "Cross-national perspectives about weight-based bullying in youth: nature, extent and remedies." Pediatric Obesity. vol. 11, Issue 4, August 2016: 241–250, 6 JUL 2015, DOI: 10.1111/ijpo.12051.

26 Puhl, Rebecca M. "Stigma, Obesity, and the Health of the Nation's Children." Psychological Bulletin, 2007, vol. 133, no. 4, 557-80. American Psychological Association.

27 Goyal M, Singh S, Sibinga EMS, Gould NF, Rowland-Seymour A, Sharma R, Berger Z, Sleicher D, Maron DD, Shihab HM, Ranasinghe PD, Linn S, Saha S, Bass EB, Haythornthwaite JA. Meditation Programs for Psychological Stress and Well-beingA Systematic Review and Meta-analysis. JAMA Intern Med. 2014;174(3):357–368. doi:10.1001/jamainternmed.2013.13018

Made in the USA
Monee, IL
06 April 2022